Legitimate Pursuit

Legitimate Pursuit
The Case for the Sporting Gun

by
Tony Jackson

**Published in association with the
British Association for Shooting and Conservation**

Ashford Press Publishing
Southampton
1988

Published by   Ashford Press Publishing 1988
               1 Church Road
               Shedfield
               Hampshire SO3 2HW

© Tony Jackson 1988

British Library Cataloguing in Publication Data
Jackson, Tony 1937 –
    Legitimate pursuit: the case for the sporting gun.
    1. Sporting firearms.   Use
    I. Title
    683.4'2

    ISBN 1 85253 104 5

Printed in Great Britain by A. Wheaton & Co. Ltd, Exeter

This book is dedicated to the sporting and target shooters of Britain and to the associations, particularly the BASC, who do so much to ensure that their sports – their legitimate pursuits – are protected and promoted.

Contents

List of illustrations (between pp 48 and 49)

Acknowledgements

The author and publishers are grateful to the following for permission to use pictures:

Richard Mason for picture 1; Hull Cartridge Co. for pictures 2, 4 and 5; B.W. Pacey for picture 6; David T. Grewcock for pictures 8, 10 and 11; Edwin M. Grant for picture 9.

Acknowledgements

1
Sporting Guns – the Background

Man will always be a hunter. For hundreds of thousands of years, long, long before recorded history, the knife, spear, net and pit-fall sustained the species which we know as Man. It is a heritage which we cannot deny, nor should we attempt to do so. Today, few of us have actually to hunt for our meat out of necessity, but those of us who enjoy and understand shooting for sport are well aware that we are continuing the tradition of the centuries, a tradition too deeply imbued in our bones to be lightly cast aside. Somewhere, sometime, in those primitive days, was borne pleasure in the chase, an instinct which even today can, if required, be turned to vital use.

Those of us who are able to use a gun or a rifle and who know how to deal with our quarry for the larder, have an innate advantage over the more 'civilised' members of society. Pragmatic in our approach to wildlife and the countryside, our apparent dichotomy of interest is easily resolved by our understanding of, and involvement in, the countryside.

In Britain, the gun as an instrument of sport, was a relative latecomer to the scene. The spear and the bow had been the instruments of the chase from Norman times, with the falcon adding a refinement to these coarser tools. Indeed, the first record of the use of trained hawks in Britain is in AD 940, in the reign of Ethelred, though hawking and falconry had both been practised in classical times.

But it was the combination of chemicals to be known eventually as gunpowder which was to change the art of warfare and, ultimately, sport. It is simply not known from whence or where the first gunpowder came, though it seems likely that it was brought back from the Far East, perhaps China, where experiments had long been carried out. All that is known for certain is that the English monk, Roger Bacon, was aware of gunpowder around 1250. It is likely that the earliest attempts to produce a gun took place simultaneously in more than one country, though the Continent, perhaps Italy or Germany, is the feasible birthplace.

Certainly the first reference to a gun appears in 1326 when two gentlemen were appointed by the Council of Florence to manufacture 'missiles or iron bullets and metal cannon'. In the same year there is depicted in an English manuscript, written for Edward III, what appears to be a vase-shaped gun firing an arrow for the purposes of siege.

What terrifying weapons those early guns must have been – less so perhaps for the intended victims as for the unfortunate gunners who had to fire them! Powder was unstable and the metal of the cannon prone to faults and weakness so that one-armed artillerymen must have been a common sight!

The first hand-held guns had either to be rested on a tripod, pressed under one arm or balanced on a shoulder, rather like a modern bazooka, whilst a lighted match, a piece of cord soaked in a solution of saltpetre or the lees of wine to make it burn slowly, was applied to the vent. An early drawing depicts a knight in armour on horseback clutching a tube to his chest, the barrel supported in a crutch propped against his groin. In his right hand is a glowing match. The recoil must have done little for his manhood or chest!

Slowly, over the years, necessity and the realisation that the gun had come to stay created a demand to improve both cannons and hand-guns. By the latter part of the 15th century a trigger, spring and sear lever had been invented, whilst the stock had assumed a shape suitable for retention against the shoulder. Ignition was by a simple match-holder known as a serpentine.

It was not until the reign of Charles II that in Britain the gun came into its own as a sporting weapon. Hitherto the hound and the falcon dominated the sporting scene and the gun was looked upon very much as a tool of the working or peasant classes. Doubtless, though, guns had been used throughout much of the 15th and 16th centuries to augment the larder. In those distant days the Fens of the eastern counties must have swarmed with fowl and it takes little imagination to picture a discharged soldier, armed with his matchlock, cutting a swathe through a flock of resting duck on a lonely dyke. Pellets or shot would have been small cubes cut from sheet lead and, whilst crude, would have been effective. This was not a time for the ethics of sportsmanship; the goal was simply to kill as many birds as possible for the pot.

On the Continent sporting shooting was well in advance of Britain and as early as 1515 edicts were being published deploring the use of guns for sporting purposes as game was already being depleted. The first rifled weapons must have been made at the end of the 15th century, for target competitions at ranges of 200 yards were even then being held in Bavaria; as it is impossible for a ball fired from an unrifled gun to prove accurate over a few yards the implication of rifling seems proven. It is known for a fact that

Maximilian I ordered a rifled gun in about 1500.

Was it Leonardo da Vinci, that extraordinary man out of his time, who was to invent the wheel lock, a significant milestone in the story of the gun? The Germans have a claim but drawings in the Codex Atlanticus provide a strong case for the Italians. The wheel lock was, for the first time, a gun capable of providing instant discharge at the behest of the user; however it was a complicated and costly piece of mechanism which could be afforded only by the very wealthy who would also embellish their guns with expensive and ornate decoration, as witnessed by the examples still to be seen today. The action of the lock was ingenious and a far cry from the simple matchlock. A serrated wheel was wound back against a spring until it came into frictional contact with a piece of iron pyrites held in the jaws of a cock. On release of the tension a shower of sparks fell into the pan, already primed with powder, to explode the main charge in the breech.

The point about the wheel lock is that it established the principle for the snaphaunce or snaplock which, in a refined form was to appear as the flintlock, a form of ignition which was used well into the 19th century, and which in itself created sporting shooting as we know it today.

The flint gun was elegant, slender and could provide, in its later form, almost certain, instant ignition. For the sport of shooting it proved a major advancement. The mechanics were simple. A flint, clamped in the jaws of a cock, working against a spring, and on being released by the trigger struck sparks from a steel which also incorporated a pan cover to keep the priming intact and dry.

In the hands of gunmakers, such as Durs Egg and Joe Manton, the flintlock assumed its final and most exquisite form. Knowledgeable sportsmen, such as Col. Peter Hawker, although resigned to the neater efficiency of the percussion lock, always regretted the departure of the flint. Even in 1854, when the breechloader had already been introduced, he wrote 'though, like the rest of the sporting world, I have long been kidnapped into the use of detonators, I have no reason to alter the opinion I gave in 1822 and, were my time to come again, I would probably be content with the flint'.

In the 18th century, 'shooting flying' using flintlocks was not just a happy accident but a regular practice. Walking behind pointers, sportsmen could tramp the long scythe-cut stubbles, flintlocks at the ready, seeking coveys of partridges or the odd pheasant. Most shots taken would be at going-away or crossing birds, for the oncoming bird would be fairly unusual.

It was a period of leisurely, even-paced sport which was to be changed by the invention of the percussion or detonator system. First instigated in 1807 by the Rev. Alexander John Forsyth (1768-1843), of Belhevie, Scotland, through the striking of fulminate, it was the invention of the copper cap which was firmly to set the percussion gun on the map. Who actually invented the cap has long been in dispute; claimants for the honour include Peter Hawker himself, the gunmaker Durs Egg, Mr Purdey, and a Joshua Shaw from America. All we know for certain is that the earliest patent was granted to a Frenchman, François Prelat.

The laborious business of loading was to remain the same, even if the means of ignition had been improved. The sportsman still had to carry powder, shot, wads and now caps, and whilst it was claimed that the infantryman could get off three shots in a minute from his Brown Bess smoothbore, the sportsman had no need to try and achieve such a rate of fire. That is, until the advent of the battue, another import from France.

For much of the first two or three decades of the 19th century shooting for sport had tended to be a relatively solitary exercise. One suspects that there was a deep conflict between the 'old school' of sportsmen, who were prepared to work for their shooting, and the *nouveau riche* approach from those who saw the battue, or driven shoot as we would call it today, as a social exercise and simply wished to entertain on a lavish scale. Even today, a not dissimilar attitude prevails between covert shooters and rough shooters, though without the animosity which formerly prevailed.

The next major developement was, of course, the introduction of the breechloader in 1851. The word 'introduction' is used deliberately as there had previously been several attempts, none of them really satisfactory. Even as early as 1812 a French patent had been taken out for a genuine breechloading system, but it was ahead of its time and overlooked. The Continent, it seemed, was a seething cauldron of ideas and inventions – the Robert breechloader, the Chateauvilliers and Dreyse needle-guns, had all been brought out prior to 1851, the year of the Great Exhibition, but none had been exploited.

There, at the Great Exhibition, that remarkable display of man's ingenuity, held in the Crystal Palace in Hyde Park, was to be seen exhibit No. 1308, a pin-fire breechloading shotgun made by Lefaucheux of Paris. An alert gunmaker, one E. C. Hodges, made a copy of the gun which he sold to Joseph Lang of Cockspur Street, and thus was born the first practical British breechloading shotgun.

4

The pin-fire system was to be relatively short-lived due to the inherent danger of the system. The basic problem was that the pin, which extruded from the base of the cartridge at right-angles and, when struck by the hammer, exploded the powder in the cartridge, was liable to accidental discharge, if dropped or accidentally struck while being carried in the pocket or cartridge bag.

However, a basic principle had been established and it was now simply a case of modification. 'Simply' is perhaps the wrong word. For the next two or three decades the gunmaking world bubbled and fermented with inventions, some grotesque, others designed ultimately to evolve into the shotgun as we know it today.

Until the early 1880s the hammergun was to dominate the field, though the first true hammerless gun was introduced in 1871. This was the Murcott system, a gun which was cocked internally by means of an under-lever which also opened the barrels.

The British gun trade quickly recognised the innovative nature of this system and modifications soon tumbled forth, not the least of which was the Anson & Deeley patent of 1875, which was to become the basic action for the boxlock hammerless shotgun. The tumbler, striker and hammer were combined into one unit, which, whilst opening the breech and dropping the barrels, cocked the locks.

In the same year the ejector system had been invented by Needham and was quickly adopted by Greener, amongst others, whilst in 1880 the gunmaker Beesley designed lockwork which was to be set on either side of the breech to produce the elegant lines of what was to be known as the sidelock.

All the elements of the sporting shotgun had now been assembled. The 'best' game gun, as we now know it, a sidelock ejector, has scarcely altered in its essentials for a century. The addition of rebounding locks and self-opening action have ensured that it remains the quintessence of perfection, the ultimate game gun. The boxlock was quickly to be recognised as the workhorse, more suited with its bulkier and simple lockwork to the harsher rigours of the marsh and rough shooting, a position which it retains today.

Meanwhile, in the New World shotgun development was setting out on a very different path, but one which met the demands of a young, tough country still in the throes of expansion. Whilst the West was being tamed by Col. Colt and Winchester, with their repeating arms, attempts were being made to provide the shotgun with an equal ability to fire a succession of shots without reloading.

One of the first production samples was simply a shotgun version of the Colt revolving-chambered rifle, but it had the inherent disadvantage of burning the shooter's forward arm as flame spurted from the cylinder, and was, understandably, not over popular.

The first really successful repeating shotgun was the Spencer slide-action, a patent on which was granted in 1882, with production beginning the following year at Windsor, Connecticut. The gun worked well, the breech mechanism being operated by a short hard rubber handle; however, initially it found little favour and the company ran into financial problems, being bought out by a Francis Bannerman. He continued production and about 20,000 of these shotguns were made.

The year 1893 saw the introduction into the market of the first Winchester pump-action, based on a clever and simple design produced by John M. Browning. In four years of production over 34,000 were sold, but it took a court case brought by Bannerman for patent infringements against Winchester, a case which he ultimately lost, to ensure the lasting popularity of the Winchester gun.

Further developments were on the way and, in 1897, one of the most popular pump-actions of all time saw the light of day. For 60 years the Winchester '97 was produced, finally ceasing in 1957, by which time nearly one million had been made.

One other competitor was to appear on the scene – Marlin, the company which had been successfully making repeating lever-action rifles in competition with Winchester. Their first pump-action shotgun appeared in 1897 and continued, with a wide range of variations, until 1934.

All these early pump-actions had an external hammer, but a new trend was introduced in 1904 with the Stevens Model 520; designed by Browning, in this gun the entire breech mechanism was enclosed within the receiver. Remington brought out its Model 10 in 1907, and in 1912 there appeared the famous Winchester Model 12; a year later Marlin struck back with its Model 28. The slide-action shotgun now dominated the USA shotgun shooting scene and can truly be said to be the all-time American shotgun, beloved of duck and goose hunters and also used extensively by clay shooters for skeet and trap.

Today there is a wide range of models available, including Winchester, Stevens, Remington, Ithaca, Browning and Mossberg. Chamber capacities are for 3, 4 or 5 cartridges but it should be noted that as far as Britain is concerned the law as it stands at the time of publication allows only a 3-shot capacity. If a pump has the ability to take 4 or 5 cartridges a plug, allowing only 3, must be inserted.

In Britain pump- or slide-action shotguns are less popular than auto-leaders. However, those who shoot them claim that they are fast and once the knack of handling the slide is acquired are excellent guns for pigeon shooting, wildfowling or clay shooting.

The auto-loader, or semi-auto, as it has come to be termed, is another excellent sporting shotgun which has earned its medals on the clay range and in the field.

The semi-automatic shotgun was conceived and designed by the famous John M. Browning in 1889 when he was 34. A unique design, Browning took it to Liege in Belgium at the turn of the century following a dispute with Winchester. The value of the concept was at once recognised and received with acclaim by the Directors of Fabrique Nationale d'Armes de Guerre. On March 24, 1902 a contract was signed giving F.N. exclusive world rights . Any doubts about the gun's possible success were quickly squashed when, in the first year of production, 10,000 models of the Browning semi-auto were sold.

Produced initially by F.N. and then by Remington and the Browning Arms Company, the semi-auto has proved to be one of the most popular sporting arms ever invented. Total production numbers are impossible to estimate, but the figure runs into millions.

Amongst the numerous variations offered it is interesting to note a 3-shot version, the Model 11, which was introduced in 1931.

The famous Browning Automatic-5 is still in production and offered in 72 different specifications. It has been copied by many manufacturers including Savage, Franchi and Breda.

2
The Sporting Shotgun

The basic principle in the use of all shotguns, irrespective of their type, remains the same. A cartridge containing a propellant, a percussion cap, wadding and shot, is loaded into the breech of the gun, by hand or mechanical means. When the breech is closed and the gun is cocked, upon being fired a firing-pin strikes the cap, which in turn detonates the charge of powder. Gases released force the load of shot through the barrel of the gun to its target.

The shotgun is essentially a smoothbore, short-range arm whose normal purpose is to fire a cartridge containing pellets at either sporting quarry or clay targets. It can also be used to fire a single rifled slug cartridge; this is usually used against wild boar or deer at close quarters.

Shotguns are then categorised by bore size. The method is simple. A 12-bore, for example, has a barrel whose size is equivalent to a ball, twelve of which weigh one pound; so a 20-bore equates to 20 balls weighing a pound, a 28-bore to 28 balls and so on. The exception is the fourteen whose bore diameter is .410 in.

Types of shotgun

These principles established, let's examine the several types of shotgun. There are five categories to be considered.

1. The single-barrel shotgun taking a single cartridge, i.e. the Greener GP.

2. The side-by-side gun.

3. The over-and-under gun.

4. The single-barrel pump-action gun.

5. The single-barrel semi-auto, gas or recoil-operated gun.

1 Single-barrel
Examples of the single-barrel shotgun are the Greener GP gun. Notable for its strength and balance due to the rearward displacement of the weight, the GP employs the famous Martini loading system incorporating an under-lever which lowers the breech plate

and allows one to insert a cartridge. It is a simple, reliable mechanism which seems rarely to be seen today, though at one time it was very popular with rough shooters and wildfowlers.

The bolt-action shotgun uses the principle employed in bolt-action rifles. It is an unsatisfactory system with a gun purporting to be a shotgun; the weight distribution is too far forward and, inevitably, one is given the impression that one is using a rifle, causing the shooter to poke the gun rather than swing it.

2   Side-by-side

The side-by-side shotgun is the game shooter's gun, though it will also be used by rough shooters and wildfowlers. The breech mechanism incorporates either external hammers – these are now rarely seen or used – or the hammerless system, whereby the hammers are a part of the lockwork. These last will be either boxlock or sidelock. In the former, a robust, simple system, the lock is set beneath the breech, giving it a square, bulky appearance, whilst the locks on a sidelock are set on either side of the breech to provide a smooth, flowing outline.

Side-by-side hammerless guns will be either ejectors or non-ejectors and there will be one or two triggers. The barrels are opened by a lever, set on top of the breech, which is moved to the right. If the gun has a self-opening action the barrels drop quickly, allowing one to reload at speed. This is essential if one is shooting driven game.

Barrels will be 25 in to 32 in, though the standard length for game guns today is 28 in. (Note that at present guns with barrels shorter than 24 in require a firearm's certificate.) Stocks can be straight hand (standard with game guns), or half or full pistol grip. These last two are more usual with guns intended for rough shooting or wildfowling.

Barrels are bored to produce a degree of choke. This is a subject which causes a great deal of confusion.

Choke is, quite simply, the degree of constriction at the end of the barrel which causes the shot charge to be compressed so that the emerging pellets spread less in their flight and produce a smaller diameter pattern at a given distance. Imagine a hosepipe being squeezed so that the jet of water is forced into a narrow stream. There are degrees of choke or restriction so that patterns of shot, as shown on the pattern plate at a distance of 30 yards, will vary from true cylinder, in which there is no degree of choke, through improved cylinder, quarter, half, three-quarter and full choke. The ballistic effect of choke is to extend the effective range of a gun, but at the same time as the pattern is increasingly constricted in full choke, the demands on the shooter's skill and accuracy are progressively extended.

Most game in this country is shot between 25 and 35 yards and the less choke employed in a game gun, the greater the allowance for a margin of error. There is an increased likelihood of missing a partridge at 25 yards with full choke, whilst if it is hit the bird will most probably be badly smashed as it will be struck by far too many pellets.

It will be found that most game guns are choked to improved cylinder in the right barrel, which is the one normally fired first when the quarry is likely to be at its closest to the shooter, and half choke in the left. This system provides the game shooter with the option of using either barrel for quarry at different distances, a benefit which is not available to the user of a single-barrel, pump-action, or semi-auto shotgun.

3 Over-and-under

With this type of shotgun the barrels are superimposed. It is, without question, the most popular gun for clay shooting in Britain, and justifiably so. The action may be boxlock or sidelock, triggers can be double, single or single selective, the top rib can be ventilated, flat or stepped and there are numerous variations available for the stock and fore-end. The latter may be beavertail, splinter or schnabel.

For game shooting the over-and-under is at a disadvantage when it comes to loading. The side-by-side requires almost half the effort required to open it, and in some over-and-unders the gap is so narrow when the gun is opened that the barrels have to be forced down to enable one to insert two cartridges. Whilst of no consequence when clay shooting, where speed is not normally essential, except during a flush shoot, it can be a significant deterrent when shooting driven birds.

However, the claims of the over-and-under for clay shooting are outstanding. The narrow, single-sighting plane is an advantage as it does not obstruct the target, whilst the heat haze above the barrel (produced by firing a quantity of cartridges), which may distort the target, will be reduced; the fore-end which encloses the barrels, prevents the foreward hand from becoming burnt; recoil is better absorbed and the construction of the gun is singularly robust. Large numbers of cartridges can be fired without too much discomfort to the shooter.

4 Pump-action

Very popular in the USA, the pump-action, slide-action or trombone action has never really caught on in Britain. Normally designed to fire five cartridges but can take up to eight; the spent cartridge is ejected and the gun recocked by pushing the fore-end back and forth. The problem with the pump is poor disposition of weight which tends to be too far forward, whilst many shooters find the action of reloading upsets their sight picture.

5 Semi-autos

The semi-auto is operated by either recoil or gas from a fired cartridge. It should be made clear that the gun can be fired only as fast as the trigger can be pulled. It cannot fire in bursts. This type of shotgun is popular with many clay shooters who find that the recoil is noticeably reduced. Lady shooters, or beginners who are nervous of recoil, will discover that a 20-bore semi-auto will enormously boost their confidence.

Semi-autos are divided into recoil-operated and gas-operated. The former has variations; the long recoil and short recoil exemplified by the F. N. Browning five and two shot semi-autos. In the former the barrels recoils 3 in, in the latter about ¾ in.

The gas-operated semi-auto diverts part of the gas from the expended cartridge into a cylinder in the fore-end. This contains a piston which works the breech mechanism.

Cartridges are ejected from the side of the action in semi-autos and when not in use the bolt must always be held back to show that the gun is unloaded. There is a wide range of options for the clay shooter, including floating, fixed, solid or ventilated ribs, straight hand or pistol grips, Monte Carlo stocks or sloping combs. Cartridges are ejected from the side of the breech.

The problem with semi-autos is that their weight distribution tends to be poor and they usually weigh between 7 lb and 8 lb. They are also prone to malfunction and can be choosy over ammunition.

Cartridges

The majority of shotgun cartridges used today are plastic cased. Formerly paper cases were exclusively employed, and whilst being in many ways more pleasant to handle and also having the added advantage of being biodegradable, they were a menace in wet or damp weather when the cases would invariably swell. The only problem with plastic cartridges is a tendency to a build-up of static so that the case becomes attractive to small particles of dirt; plastic cases must also be retrieved once they have been fired.

The cartridge is a closed tube, designed to fit inside the chamber of a gun, with a flange at the base. This last consists of a brass or steel head into which the percussion cap is set. Today caps are non-corrosive. The purpose of the cap, when struck by the firing-pin, is to detonate the main charge of powder with a flash of flame.

Separating the powder from the shot or charge of pellets is a wad. Only the home-loader or clay specialist need really concern himself today with brands of powder. Modern nitro powders are either fibrous or gelatinised compounds which, it is important to note, are not in themselves explosive. Modern smokeless powders are manufactured with varying characteristics, ranging from fast burning to produce high velocity loads to slow burning for progressive powders behind heavy loads. There was a time when the shooter would require to know what type of powder a cartridge contained, as pressures and results varied considerably, and storage was an important factor, especially if they were being used in hot climes, but today he can rely on the consistency and reliability of powders, provided he uses well-known brands.

Wads are normally constructed of plastic, though felt or fibre still has its adherents, particularly with skeet shooters who look for wide patterns. Modern plastic wads, too, tend to throw patterns which are slightly tighter than those thrown by fibre wads. The old Eley 'Kleena' was always a great favourite as it helped to prevent leading of the barrels. Leading is the greyish streaks left in a barrel after firing and which, if not removed, will eventually cause pitting.

The chief purpose of the wad is to act as a seal between the shot charge and the hot, powerful gases driving it through the barrel. Should any gas escape into the charge the result may be a fusion of the pellets, known as 'balling' which can be highly dangerous, or at the very least produce badly blown or distributed patterns. So much depends on the quality of the wadding.

The shot itself consists of spherical lead pellets. These may be nickel-plated to increase hardness and to ensure even patterns through the elimination of deformed pellets. Shot is still made in the traditional fashion by dropping the molten metal from a high tower through a current of cold air, the resultant pellets being known as 'chilled' shot.

Pellets are graded into varying sizes according to the purpose for which they are required. Each size is designated by a numeral or letter. Unfortunately, there is no consistency of numbering world-wide. British shot sizes range from the smallest size, No. 9 down through 7, 6, 5, 4, 3 and 1, to the large lettered shot such as BB, AAA, SSG.

For game most shooters prefer No. 6 or No. 7 shot. An ounce of No. 6, for instance, contains 270 pellets, whilst an ounce of No. 7

some 340 pellets. Shot loads vary according to the size and bore of the gun and its proofing. A 20-bore chambered for a 3 in cartridge will fire 1⅜ oz of shot, i.e. 371 pellets of No. 6. A .410 shotgun chambered for the 2 in cartridge will fire a load of only ½ oz containing 135 pellets of No. 6.

The beginner or novice usually imagines that the heavier the load and the more pellets he can get into the air, the greater his chances of connecting with his target. However, experience will show that the majority of all-round game shooters in this country, dealing with a variety of driven and going-away birds, find that they can maintain an excellent average with a 1 oz or 1¹/₁₆ oz load of No. 6 or 7 shot.

All guns have to be nitro-proved before they can be sold in Britain. There are two proof houses, one in Birmingham, the other in London. When a gun, either new or second-hand, is sent for proof, it is subject to a test which will disclose any fault. If the gun passes then proof marks are stamped on the flats of the barrel. This practice is a sensible precaution observed by most European gun manufacturers. One notable exception is the USA which has no proof test.

The lethal characteristics of a shotgun are frequently a cause of misunderstanding, not just amongst those who have little or nothing to do with guns or firearms, but also those just starting in shooting. The problem lies partially in the fact that the shotgun is used largely for bird shooting and there is, therefore, a curious mental reluctance to appreciate that it can also be used to kill a human. There is a dichotomy of purpose, made no easier by the tendency to refer to it as a scattergun, a word which emphasises several misconceptions. Certainly pellets begin to disperse the moment they leave the barrel, but their velocity is such that they still retain a coherent form until they reach 50 or 60 yards when they do, indeed, begin to scatter, as we understand the term. There is no such misunderstanding with a rifle which, because of its close association with warfare in the public eye, always assumes a totally lethal property, irrespective of its calibre or its ammunition.

It must always be borne in mind, therefore, that whilst shotguns may be employed mostly against birds, or in breaking clays, both under controlled, civilised conditions, when fired at close range, say zero to 20 yards, a shotgun can easily kill a human. A charge of shot, containing perhaps 270 pellets of No. 6, will mangle and blow apart bones, flesh, arteries and nerve ends. If struck in the trunk at close range death is nearly certain, whilst if a limb is hit it will mean amputation. It is hardly surprising that the shotgun is frequently chosen as a close-encounter weapon under battle conditions. There is little to choose between borings where close quarter encounters take place. A .410 can be just as devastating as a 12-bore, even though it is frequently treated as a boy's gun, almost on a par with an air-gun.

Any big game hunter, too, will tell you that he prefers to carry a shotgun, loaded with heavy letter shot, if he has to follow up a wounded leopard. He will probably have only a split second to fire at very close range, and he knows that a shotgun offers far greater protection than a rifle.

Beginners should always be given a demonstration of the terrifying effects of a shotgun at close quarters. The message can be driven home if a tin containing water is fired at from 10 yards. The target will virtually explode when the charge hits it.

But don't be misled into thinking that damage to the human frame is only likely at close range. A pellet can still put out an eye at 200 yards.

One might suppose then that shooting accidents would be commonplace in this country. It is after all a relatively small, densely populated island. Throughout the shooting season hundreds of thousands of sportsmen are out, a few shooting perhaps two or three days a week from August through the winter till the end of January, whilst clay shooting takes place every week of the year. Millions of cartridges are fired in the field and on the range, yet it is a fact that shooting accidents are very, very uncommon.

Where gun safety is concerned Britain, I would suggest, leads the world. Shooting men in this country have a reputation for setting the highest standards, both as sportsmen and for safety in the field and on the clay range. Whilst we have a natural advantage as a nation, tending to be less volatile, more calm and phlegmatic than, say, some of our more excitable Continental neighbours, we also owe an enormous debt to both the British Association for Shooting & Conservation (BASC) and the Clay Pigeon Shooting Association (CPSA), each of whom has laid enormous emphasis over the years on gun safety. Shooting men in Britain have always been brought up in a tradition which has demanded the exercise of the highest standards. Nothing less will do. Anyone who transgresses the safety laws of the shooting field on a regular basis will swiftly find himself devoid of friends and shooting.

For many years BASC has provided demonstrations on gun safety at country fairs and sporting occasions and published a set of rules to be adhered to at all times. The CPSA, too, places heavy emphasis on gun safety, being well aware that target shooting usually takes place in front of an audience, and often at public occasions. Beginners, too, in their hundreds, are coached and taught at country fairs, yet there is never a hint of danger. The rules are closely observed and anyone breaching them is jumped on at once.

At this point an explanation of the theory of shooting may help to dispell some of the myths which have built up around the sport, largely created by a media wholly ignorant of the world of guns and firearms.

From time immemorial sporting journalists have waited with weary resignation for the opening of the grouse season, the only shooting date in the calendar known to the popular media. For the week or so following August the world will be regaled with tales of rifles cracking on the moors and tame grouse being blasted out of the sky ad nauseam. All of it is misinformation, based on ignorance and indicative of a total, and often deliberate, misunderstanding of driven shooting and the use of the sporting shotgun.

'How on earth can you miss?' is a frequent query from a usually aggressive non-shooter. 'Your cartridges are crammed with pellets and a shotgun scatters them all round the bird, so what chance does it have?' What indeed! Yet, curiously, these instant experts, if they can be persuaded to test their theories at clay pigeons, revise them within a shot or two!

To shoot at and hit a flying target, be it a bird or clay, demands a considerable degree of computerised mental agility and muscular coordination. One must make allowance for speed, whether the target is approaching, going away, crossing or rising, allow also for any drift and then, when all these factors have been absorbed, calculate how far in front one must fire in order that the shot charge and target coincide.

Theoretically, provided all these factors are correctly identified one should never miss! However, it's not quite like that. Old-fashioned shooting books would provide tables purporting to show the lead required to shoot birds flying at varying speeds. For instance, one was told that the allowance for a bird crossing at 40 mph using No. 6 shot at 35 yards would be 6ft 8in. This information was, of course, totally meaningless other than as an exercise to satisfy ballistic experts. In real life the experienced and successful shooting man is aware that the laws of ballistics demand that he shoot ahead of his moving target, whilst in practice he may only be aware of swinging at the target, although he will indeed have overshot it to the necessary amount as he pulled the trigger.

There are several schools of thought regarding style and method of shooting but these are not relevant to this book. Suffice it for the tyro to know and understand that shotgun shooting is an art, a highly specialised skill which, when demonstrated by top clay shooters or driven game shots, can be made to appear ridiculously simple. Here lies a trap for the unwary. Unaware of the complexities involved they make assumptions based on misinformation.

To show the distribution of shot from a variety of pellet sizes and loads, shots will be taken at a whitewashed plate at a measured 40 yards from the shooter. The centre of the pattern will be estimated and a 30 in circle drawn around it. The number of pellets within the circle will be counted.

It should be understood that smaller bore shotguns do not shoot smaller patterns. This is a common misconception. Thus the pattern from a 20-bore will still be the same size as that for a 12-bore but with a reduced number of pellets due to the smaller charge. So a 28-bore may place 100 pellets within the 30 in circle but a 12-bore will exactly double this number.

At 40 yards, nominal percentage patterns for all borings would show 40% for true cylinder, 50% for imp. cylinder, and up to 70% for full choke.

But pattern plates can be misleading to the untutored eye. Whilst they may present a mass of pellet strikes, there may well be large gaps through which a bird could easily fly untouched. This, when it happens, usually indicates that the barrel of the gun is badly bored and needs attention from a gunsmith in order to try and produce regular, even patterns.

It has been claimed by those with little understanding of either that the shotgun is a blunt, brute instrument in contrast to the precision of the rifle. It is an understandable attitude but one which belies the facts. To use a shotgun successfully requires the coordination of a number of skills, a fact seldom appreciated by the unknowing onlooker. The rifle shooter has a different set of calculations and adjustments, both mental and physical.

3
The Sporting Rifle

The development of the sporting rifle, like the shotgun, took place largely in mainland Europe. Rifling was already in use, as noted in Chapter 1, in the late 15th century and the rifle, whose singular feature was the grooves cut into the barrel to induce the ball to spin in flight, was advanced through the efforts of the gunmakers of Italy, notably at Brescia and Gardone in northern Italy, and those of Germany, Austria and Holland.

From the 16th century onwards the sporting rifle, in various guises, played an important role in Europe but was virtually totally neglected in Britain where there was, perhaps, less incentive in the shape of big game for its evolution. Wild boar, deer, chamois and elk were sufficient reason to ensure that there were arms capable of dealing with them, so that by the beginning of the 18th century a variety of calibres had evolved capable of coping with a diversity of game. Calibres ranged between .30 in up to a massive .70 in and game would be stalked or else driven to the rifles by a team of beaters.

In America, too, there was an obvious requirement for rifles, both for sport and for defence as the country was opened up. Pioneers lived off the land and, at the same time, had need for a rifle for protection against marauding Indians. The result was the emergence of the Kentucky rifle. A superb weapon, usually .45 inch calibre, it had an effective and accurate range up to nearly 400 yards and could make a 4 in group at 100 yards. Its effect against British soldiers in the American War of Independence was shattering; it was a typical guerilla weapon in the hands of men who knew how to use it and were capable of employing long-range tactics against a foe who still depended on mass-formation firepower. For the British Army was armed with a gun which, by virtue of its rapid rate of fire, due to simple reloading, and resistance to powder residue build-up, was effective when facing a massed foe perhaps no more than 50 or 60 yards away but hopeless as a long-range weapon. The Tower musket, or 'Brown Bess', was smooth-bored and lacked any pretensions to accuracy. The chances of deliberately hitting a human figure at 100 yards were negligible.

It was the expansion and developement of the British Empire and the special demands it made upon its adminstrators and explorers which was rapidly to create a demand for sporting weapons. It was the period of the big bore muzzle-loaders. The requirement was for a gun with massive knock-down power capable of dealing with elephant, rhino or buffalo, a demand which in turn called for penetration and killing power, both of which could be obtained only by increasing the powder charge. The problem was that in order to accommodate a heavy powder charge the guns had to be smooth-bored; if they were rifled the bullet would simply strip the rifling. In other words it travelled too fast up the barrel to grip the rifling.

These huge 4-, 6- and 8-bores lacked, however, knock-down power as can be shown by the books of the period.

Writing in his well-known work *The Lion Hunter in South Africa*, Roualeyn Gordon Cumming describes the horrendous encounters he had with elephants during the 1840s. On one occasion he fired 35 bullets into an unfortunate bull, all around the shoulder area and from a distance of 15 to 35 yards, before the beast collapsed. This was from a massive 6-bore.

The famous hunter and explorer, Courtenay Selous, too, knew the effects of the big bores. One day hunting elephant, a gun-bearer inadvertently double charged his 4-bore and he was thrown head-over-heels, and suffered a deep cut to the face as the stock burst, despite being wrapped in green elephant skin. He claimed that, as a result of this accident, he never fully recovered his health.

The developement of the two-groove rifling system by James Purdey took the big-game rifle a stage further. These weapons were single barrelled and took a relatively small charge of slow-burning powder to make sure the bullet gripped the rifling.

However, hazardous encounters with elephants, lions and buffalos soon persuaded hunters that they needed a second barrel for a quick, emergency shot. Relying on a bearer to hand over a second loaded rifle was too risky when facing a wounded animal. Thus was born the double big-game rifle, a weapon which even today has its adherents in Africa. Not intended for, nor capable of, long-range accuracy, the double was meant to be used almost like a shotgun for short-range snap shooting and as such was highly effective. It appeared in a variety of calibres such as the .577, the .500 and .475.

In Britain two other types of sporting rifle appeared. The first was a deer calibre around .60 produced to cater for the sudden enthusiasm for red deer stalking in the Scottish Highlands, fostered by the Royal Family; the other was the so-called rook rifle. This last fired a low velocity bullet of calibre. 380 down to. 255; giving little recoil and having only a limited range, it was useful for knocking over rabbits, rooks and other small game.

Meanwhile the scene switched back to the USA where, as a result of the conflict between North and South, major developments had taken place amongst armaments. In 1855 Smith & Wesson brought out the first lever-action rim-fire rifle of .50 calibre, and this was swiftly followed by the Volcanic rifle in .38 calibre, and four years later by the Henry in .44. Another rifle used in the conflict was the .54 Sharps, which later was to be developed into the famous 'buffalo' gun in .44-77 calibre.

Immediately after the American Civil War, Winchester produced their .44 rimfire. This became the Winchester '73 in centre-fire in that year, whilst Colt, in 1888, brought out the first pump-action rifle.

Back on the European Continent percussion muzzle-loaders finally gave way to breechloading rifles and a series of experiments, based on military requirements, finally threw up the action which was to become inextricably linked wth the sporting rifle. Both Mauser and Mannlicher were to design military actions, operated manually by a bolt and fed from a box or rotary-type magazine. It was a simple, satisfactory design quickly adopted by the German army.

The Model 71 was the first successful rifle designed and produced by Peter Paul Mauser and his brother Wilhelm and led, ultimately, to the famous Mauser 98 action system, through a whole series of designs.

The sporting rifle, in its several divergent forms, had now come of age.

Modern rifles

Today sporting rifles are separated into the following categories – bolt-action, lever-action, pump-action, semi-auto action, single-shot action, double-barrel and drilling types.

Bolt-action

This is really the standard, world-wide accepted action for a sporting rifle. Simple, easy to manipulate, it provides the rifle with clean, classical lines. A manually operated bolt, when pulled back and pushed forward, ejects a spent case, chambers a fresh round and cocks the action. Calibres range from the smallest – the .22 up to the heaviest, the .460 Weatherby Magnum. The bullet weight of the .22 Short rim-fire is 27 grains, that of the .460 is 500 grains! Between lies a vast range of calibres each designed for a specific purpose. In Britain today the calibres most commonly used to deal with deer are the .243, .270, .308, .30-06, 6 mm Remington and 7 × 57 Mauser.

21

For larger game abroad calibres such as the .338 and .300 Winchester Magnum, 9.3 × 74 mm, .375 Magnum, .416 Rigby, .458 Winchester and the .460 Weatherby are all in regular use.

It should be noted that two types of cartridge – the rim-fire and centre-fire – are used in Britain. The rim-fire calibres are variations of the .22 theme, with the exception of the .22 Hornet which is in centre-fire. The rim-fire bullet has the percussion compound in the rim or flange of the case, so that when struck by the hammer, it will ignite, irrespective of its position in the chamber. Extensively used for target shooting and rabbit or small game, the .22 rim-fire is not to be underestimated. Although it generates little recoil or noise, it can be a very fast bullet and maintains considerable accuracy.

For dealing with a rabbit population explosion the .22, using subsonic ammuniton, is ideal. There is scarcely more than a slight pop from the rifle, so that, with care, rabbit after rabbit can be picked off. For this sort of work a semi-auto is perfect as one does not have to keep working a bolt, a distraction which rabbits will swiftly spot.

The centre-fire bullet has the percussion cap set in the centre of the base of the case. This type of bullet has available the greatest number of calibres – at least 100.

Lever-action

This type of action is synonymous with the American Wild West. There can be few adults and children who, however ignorant they may be about rifles and guns, are not familiar with the Winchester or Henry lever-action rifle. Bullets are loaded into a tube under the barrel; depressing the lever, which is an integral part of the trigger guard, feeds a bullet into the action and cocks the external hammer. On being fired, a further depression of the lever ejects the spent case through a port in the side of the action and loads a further round.

Lever-actions are basically intended for short-range brush shooting and in the carbine versions are ideal for carrying on horseback. They are seldom encountered in Britain.

Pump-action

Curiously, whilst the pump-action shotgun is considered as the all-American gun, the rifle version has never proved so popular. Bullets are pumped into the action and spent cases ejected as the fore-end is worked back and forth. It can be a very fast-action gun in skilled hands and is available in a range of calibres from .22 to .308. Again, it is seldom seen in this country.

Semi-auto action

The semi-auto action, or auto-loader, is available in rim-fire and centre-fire, each involving a different mode of operation. In the former, in .22 calibre, the mechanism works on the recoil operated blow-back system. In the latter, reloading is activated by a portion of the gas from the fired round – the spent case is ejected, a fresh round fed into the chamber and the action cocked ready to fire.

It must be made absolutely clear that the semi-auto is precisely what its name implies. It is not capable of burst fire by holding the trigger back. Each shot requires separate pressure on the trigger. However, a full magazine can be fired very rapidly. Magazines can be obtained holding five, ten or more rounds of .22 ammunition. It is a perfect rifle for rabbit control.

Single-shot action

In .22 versions these relatively simple rifles are available in several styles – bolt-action, lever-action and break-open. They are useful as training rifles for youngsters and capable of dealing with rabbits, squirrels and other small ground game.

As a serious hunting rifle the single-shot with a falling-block action has a stalwart following, particularly amongst Americans. The famous Ruger No. 1 rifle is made in calibres from .222 Swift up to .458 Winchester and is considered to be a notably accurate rifle. Using a single-shot invokes considerable discipline on the hunter. The one shot must count, for although one can reload with reasonable speed, it is not as fast as a bolt-action. Again, seldom used in Britain.

Double-barrel

The double rifle, whilst still made in London, is extremely expensive and usually intended only for the big-game hunter abroad. The double incorporates elements which require highly experienced gunsmithing. Both barrels, for instance, must group together at 100 yards, a task which requires a knowledge not just of mechanics, but also of climates. The effects of blazing tropical heat on nitro powders can easily alter alignment calculations which, in the cold of Britain, appeared satisfactory.

Double rifles are extremely expensive, used abroad and have little significance in the sport of Britain.

Drilling

The term 'drilling' is loosely used to describe a rifle-shotgun combination of typical German or Austrian design. Its origin was to act as a jack-of-all-trades weapon to cope with the possibility of a hare or blackcock, followed almost simultaneously by a wild boar or deer. A wide variety of game, often closely encountered by the hunter, created a demand for a weapon capable of handling any contingency.

The drilling is actually a side-by-side shotgun with a rifle barrel set beneath; variations on this theme are the bockdrilling in which a shotgun barrel is superimposed on a rifle barrel; the Doppel-buchsdrilling has two rifle barrels, each perhaps of a different calibre, over a shotgun barrel, and the Vierling comprises side-by-side shotgun barrels over superimposed rifle barrels, of which the top is rim-fire and the bottom centre-fire.

The obvious problem with each of these variations is, in the heat of action, trying to recall which barrel does what!

Needless to say these combination gun/rifles are a purely Continental phenomenom.

Bullets and Calibres

For the layman rifle and shotgun cartridges are a source of endless confusion and pitfalls.

Ask the average man in the street which bullet is likely to do more damage, a large calibre or a small calibre, and he will, not unnaturally, choose the former. Yet, in fact, the reverse is often the case.

First of all, bullets can be divided into two camps – soft nosed or hard. This last category, which is fully metal cased, can be dismissed fairly quickly as it hardly concerns us, other than to know its effects and use.

A full metal-jacket bullet is, as its name implies, composed of solid metal with a lead core which is inserted from the rear. This type of bullet is used for target shooting, for military purposes, or for big game, such as buffalo or elephant, where the bullet has to drive through thick skin and bone before striking the brain, lungs or heart. With animals of this character a soft-nosed bullet would dissipate its energy as it struck skin and bone and would fail to penetrate a vital area where its main energy dissipation should take place. This type of bullet is not required for sporting purposes in this country.

The bullet normally used for all soft-skinned game has a lead core inserted in the nose and the base of the bullet is metal clad. Soft- or thin-skinned game includes all the deer and antelope species, bears and cats. To deal adequately with these animals it is essential that the bullet should enter the body, through skin and bone, and release its energy in a vital area such as the heart or lungs.

24

A soft-nose bullet achieves this necessary requirement by deforming the bullet into a mushroom shape and at the same time transferring energy to the soft tissues. Very fast expansion is needed in the case of a small animal such as a roe deer, weighing about 45 lb, so that the bullet achieves its effect inside the animal before exiting. In the case of a moose, an animal weighing about 1,000 lb plus, the bullet is required to expand at a slower rate so that it has penetrated bone and muscle before releasing its energy in a vital area.

There are numerous variations on the soft-nosed theme, each designed for a specific purpose and calibre. Some bullets have sharp points, others are rounded, whilst those intended for tubular magazine rifles have flat noses to prevent detonations in the magazine.

A great deal of misapprehension and confusion with the emotive term "dum-dum" bullets has caused some members of the public, quite unconversant with rifles, ballistics or deer, to call for a ban on soft-nosed bullets.

Such a ban would, in fact, cause immense cruelty even supposing fully metal cased bullets were given legal sanction against deer. Bullets would simply go clean through the animal, with no expansion and, unless hitting heart or lung, would merely cause horrific injuries from which the animal might later succumb through loss of blood. Even when a deer is hit in the heart with a soft-nose it may still run for a 100 or more yards. The soft-nose bullet is specifically designed to cause maximum damage to a vital organ and minimum damage to meat.

So-called varmint bullets are intended for use in high-velocity .22 rifles against animals such as foxes. The bullets are basically lead covered in a thin skin of metal. Under high-velocity they become fragile and, whilst highly effective against small animals, merely cause a terrible wound if fired at larger species, such as deer, as there is little penetration and the bullet virtually explodes on the surface.

How dangerous is a bullet fired from a sporting rifle, be it a .22 rim-fire or a .270? The answer must be *very* dangerous and anyone who tries to play down the lethal characteristics is doing the sport no service. Even the tiny pellet of lead, weighing no more than 27 or perhaps 36 grains, will carry for a mile, and can kill or cause severe injury.

However, it comes as little surprise to those of us who are involved in sporting rifle shooting, in Britain whether with deer or ground game, to learn that accidents in this field are extremely rare. A contrast to the scene in the USA where the opening of the whitetail season in New York State invariably brings a crop of deaths and injuries, all caused by a combination of ignorance and lack of self-control.

Fortunately, where firearms are concerned in Britain we have the British Deer Society, the St. Hubert Club and, of course, the BASC, each of whom lays heavy emphasis on safety in the field, the home and when travelling.

4
Sporting Shotgun Shooting in the UK

Driven Game Shooting

It can truly be said, without fear of denial, that Great Britain has the finest driven game shooting in the world. It is a fact readily acknowledged by sportsmen from abroad, many of whom return to these Isles, season after season, to shoot pheasants, grouse and partridges in the confident knowledge that the sport is organised with competence to produce classical sporting birds in the most superb scenery. Quite bluntly, our heritage of driven game shooting has set the standard which others follow but seldom match.

Certainly, you can shoot massive bags of pheasants in Hungary but the flat, unbroken plains and dull coverts cannot compete with the rich pastoral landscapes of England, the hilly slopes of Wales or the sheer magnificence of Scotland. Partridges may be killed by the hundred in Spain, and good birds they are too, but they are not the birds we know and love in Britain, skimming the hedgerows or belts under a late September sun.

It is all a question of the essential character of the day, the background and the tradition, both of which are vital aspects of any day's sport.

When did it all begin? Throughout the languid years of the 18th century, when the flintlock still prevailed, game was shot walking up behind pointers. A typical day's shooting would see perhaps two or three friends and their servants, with as many brace of pointers, leisurely working the stubbles or roots for partridges or the odd pheasant. There was pause between each shot for reloading as powder, wads and shot were rammed home, the pan fresh primed and the flint checked. Overhead shots were avoided as the priming was likely to scatter from the pan; birds were almost invariably shot going away or crossing.

Shooting was now a clearly defined sport, embracing its own set of rules and traditions, while gamekeepers and game farming were already established. It is known, for instance, that in the reign of Charles II red-legged partridges were imported from the Continent and released in Windsor Forest, whilst The Marquis of

Hertford and the Earl of Rochdale each obtained thousands of red-legged partridge eggs from France and had them set under broodies. In Ireland an Andrew Rowe of Tipperary had established a game farm in 1761, selling pheasants, partridges and wild duck.

The even tenor of this sporting life was dramatically to alter with the introduction of the detonating system through the efforts of the Rev. Alexander Forsyth. The flintlock system was gradually superceded and, whilst shotguns were still loaded from the front, it was now possible to shoot high flying, overhead birds, for there was little danger, with the percussion lock, of the copper cap falling from the nipple.

It is quite likely that driven shooting started on several estates almost simultaneously. Social entertaining on a broad scale had now become a practicality with the spread of the railway system and it was incumbent upon a host to entertain his guests. What better way than some form of shoot? Some writers suggest that the 'battue', imported from France, was the origin of driven shooting. Perhaps so, but if this is the case it was an inauspicious beginning. Sporting writers of the period mocked the early battues, which, in many ways, were simply minor reflections of the horrendous slaughters which had been a feature of 18th century sporting life on the Continent.

The excesses of that period were sickening. For instance, in 1753 a party of 23 shooters in Bohemia slew 47,950 head of game over a period of three weeks. Animals and birds were driven into net-enclosed woodland from which they could not escape; it was sport in a totally perverted and decadent form.

The battue, as R.S. Surtees so scathingly described it, was a 'timid, contrived affair unworthy of the name of sport'. Birds were usually low and coverts were completely surrounded by guns, whilst beaters were just as likely to knock birds down with sticks as let them go forward.

Times change and there is little doubt that by the time the first practical breechloader had been introduced around 1851 driven shooting was an organised sport with its own rules. By the 1890s the 12-bore shotgun had reached a perfection which, in the view of many eminent authorities, has not been surpassed. The hammerless, sidelock ejector became inextricably linked with that remarkable period in the latter part of the 19th century and the Edwardian years when driven shooting passed through its Golden Age.

The ground rules for the driven shoot as we know it today, whether for pheasants, partridges or grouse, were well established.

It was agreed that the side-by-side gun, which had been developed specifically for driven shooting, met all the requirements; aesthetically pleasing, it handled well due to perfect balance, was light and unlikely to tire the shooter who might fire a hundred or more cartridges in a day, and had the inestimable advantage of a provision for instant choice of choke when shooting. Two, and sometimes even three guns with appropriate loaders were often used in those distant days and even now, whilst less common, there are still occasions when two guns and a loader are required. This will be the case when grouse shooting and a large bag is expected, or on a driven day for pheasants when the bag may exceed 300 or 400 birds.

The serious driven game man will always prefer to have a pair of guns available, exactly matched. Even if he seldom has call to use them as a pair, should one gun be incapacitated, for whatever reason, he has the other readily available.

Today, driven pheasant shooting is the backbone to shooting in Britain. Relatively simple to rear and release, pheasants provide excellent sport provided they are shown correctly. Driven pheasant shoots, at whatever level, are widely established throughout Britain and the sport is becoming increasingly popular, particularly with businessmen, many of whom now live in the country, although they may still work in cities.

A complete industry has grown up around driven shooting. Game farmers, keepers, the gun trade, cartridge manufacturers, clothing companies, kennels – all supply and maintain an important and vital countryside activity. The Game Conservancy, the body which undertakes such valuable research work, can, with its rapidly expanding membership, now approaching 20,000, testify to the increasingly important role played in the conservation and ecology of the countryside by driven shooting.

Pressure on farmers to maintain headlands and hedges, copses and coverts, comes principally because of shootings' interest. At the end of the day there may be a motive of self-interest as far as the shooting man is concerned, but he has the satisfaction of knowing that a genuine beneficiary of his sport is wildlife in general.

Rough Shooting

Thousands of shooting men (and women) derive enormous satisfaction from the less formal and simpler pleasures of rough shooting. Often they are deeply interested in gundogs and the sheer joy of working their animals for a relatively small bag provides a deep and lasting pleasure. There are shoots by the score of perhaps only a few hundred acres or less which simply do not lend themselves to driven shooting, but are ideal for a day's pottering. The bag may be only a brace of pheasants, a few rabbits and a pigeon or two but every shot will have been recalled with pleasure when driven days have long faded from memory.

For the rough shooter, too, there is always the chance of the unexpected bonus; a sudden fall of woodcock in November or a spring of teal exploding from a tiny pond, a marsh suddenly alive with snipe, or golden plover flighting back and forth. And if he lives in Scotland he may have access to one of those wonderful pieces of ground beloved of blackgame or capercaillie, blue hares and grouse.

The rough shooter must work for his sport. But he will have the benefit of being close to nature and, if he does some modest amateur keepering, he will know the cycles of the year. Some shoots are fortunate to have natural water; on others ponds can be created. A rough shoot with water can be a sheer joy as those who have flighted wild duck or teal at dusk, heard snipe drumming and occasional geese flighting over, can testify.

The rough shooter's armoury can be varied. If he is solitary and prefers to shoot alone or with one companion he may choose a semi-auto or a pump-action. Both guns are useful if he wants to maximise his chances. A pack of mallard coming in to a flash on the water meadows may call, he feels, for a quick three shots. Under Schedule 2, Part 1 of the Wildlife and Countryside Act effectively only 3 shots may be loaded for wildfowl, woodcock, snipe, golden plover and capercaillie. Remember that either gun, with its legal maximum of three shots, has the ability to deal swiftly with a cripple. A wounded duck which falls into water will quickly dive and swim to cover, sometimes baffling even the best canine duck hunter, but a quick third shot as it hits the water will settle the matter.

For the majority of rough shooters, though, the side-by-side or over-and-under is the standard gun, whether it be a boxlock or sidelock. The gun used for driven shooting can also be used for rough shooting, though the majority will prefer to keep their 'best' gun(s) for a sport which is unlikely to bring it to any harm; most rough shooters choose a gun which they know will stand up to some rough-and-tumble. The hazards of barbed wire and clambering over ditches and fences, are best catered for with a workmanlike gun. A scratch on the stock of a Purdey may bring on a mild coronary but a modest boxlock so disfigured is of little account.

Wildfowling

The wildfowler is a specialist (and in the view of some more effete shooters also a masochist!). His sport is mainly below the sea wall or inland on stretches of open water where the duck and geese are totally wild. If he shoots flight ponds or inland splashes he is a rough or duck shooter but he is not a wildfowler.

Only those who have experienced the joys of wildfowling can know and understand the sport. It is one of the last truly wild sports left in this country; the birds have never known the hand of man and are truly free while the odds are greatly pitted against the 'fowler'. He is seeking his quarry in their natural element and has to adapt accordingly. He is bound by the constraints of weather, wind and tide – they may act for him or against him. Always, too, there is the added hazard of danger to life. Only a fool plays games with the sea and, if he does, it is only once.

By its very nature it is a solitary sport, though, for reasons of sheer self-protection, wildfowlers have had to organise themselves through a system of clubs covering virtually every accessible fowling spot on the British coast. Formerly owing allegiance to the Wildfowlers' Association of Great Britain and Ireland (WAGBI), they now mostly belong to the British Association for Shooting & Conservation, the national shooting body which developed from WAGBI.

For such a sport, undertaken in muddy, wet, salt-ridden conditions, only a specialist gun is suitable. Formerly, the big bores were accepted as the wildfowler's guns; 4-bores, 8- and 10-bores firing heavy loads were considered almost essential for successful sport. Times change, and though a handful of fowlers still choose to shoot 8-bores, more for nostalgic reasons than any notions of huge bags, the majority prefer a magnum 12-bore, i.e. one with a 3 in chamber to handle the heavier loads which are frequently required when dealing with geese and duck at maximum effective range.

Some experienced fowlers, however, are quite content to use a 2¾ in 12-bore. Sometimes, but not often, duck may be flighting almost on top of a hidden gunner. I recall one occasion when, lying up in a gutter on a tide flight I had teal literally buzzing round my head but, because they were so close, I found that my heavy 3 in magnum was worse than useless. It was the sort of occasion when a light 20-bore would have been ideal.

Having said that, a balance must be struck; most fowlers prefer a heavy, magnum boxlock built on simple, unadorned lines. There is no place on the foreshore for figured walnut or fancy engraving. Some fowlers chose a semi-auto to give them that extra quick shot but the ever present danger of sand and mud too often leads to jammed actions.

Pigeon and Vermin

Like the wildfowler, the dedicated pigeon shooter is a true specialist. Today, due largely to an altered pattern of farming, the consistent big bags, which were a feature of pigeon shooting in the 1960s, are rarely encountered. Shooters will still take the odd hundred or more off oil-seed rape, peas, seed or laid barley, but pigeon seem now to be increasingly wary and fickle in their choice of fare.

Shooting over decoys is still the big killer, whilst roost shooting will probably provide the finest sport of all as the birds stream in to the bare February woodlands at all angles. For roost shooting a standard game gun with the usual game load of an ounce or $1^{1}/_{16}$ oz shot will work wonders. It was once almost an article of faith that pigeon could only be killed with heavy shot, such as No. 4 or 5. The theory was that the breast feathers provided a downy armour-plating! However, there are few pigeon which will not fold up satisfactorily if struck by a pattern of 6s or 7s!

Again, for decoy shooting a game gun, side-by-side or over-and-under, is perfectly adequate. However, many serious decoy shooters find that the semi-auto is an excellent gun for this sport. There is every chance of taking three birds out of a flock as they drop in to the decoy pattern, or killing a cripple with that extra third shot. Another consideration is that if one is lucky enough to hit a day when the pigeon are streaming in, the reduced recoil of the semi-auto is a genuine aid to consistent shooting and means you will not end the day, having fired perhaps 100-plus cartridges, with a bruised shoulder and cheek.

The semi-auto is a thoroughly handy and efficient gun, whether it is the chosen tool of the pigeon shooter, the man who has to deal with squirrels, rabbits or winged vermin or the clay shooter.

For the keeper, amateur or professional, the semi-auto is also a workmanlike tool. It handles quickly, has that extra cartridge which can be so useful when one has to deal with several birds or animals at once, and can be relied on not to take umbrage if handled in an unceremonious fashion.

It is important to re-emphasise that the semi-auto is just that; it is not an automatic. If it were one would merely keep the trigger pressed back to fire all the cartridges. It is an error which is constantly being made by those who should know better. The author of a book on shooting recently published continually and mistakenly refers to automatic shotguns when he means semi-autos.

Clay Shooting

Whilst the over-and-under is, without question, the most popular type of shotgun used for clay shooting in Britain today, in second place must come the semi-auto.

Clay shooting is a highly specialised sport, one recognised by the Olympic Committee, and as such its several disciplines demand guns and cartridges of a distinctive nature.

The beginner may be surprised to realise that there are nine clay shooting disciplines recognised in this country. They are: Down-the-Line; Double Rise; English Skeet; ISU Skeet (an Olympic discipline); English Sporting; FITASC Sporting; Olympic Trench (again an Olympic discipline); Universal Trench and Automatic Ball Trap.

To detail each individual discipline would be pointless, but suffice it to say that perhaps the most popular are English Sporting and Skeet followed by Down-the-Line. The remaining disciplines tend, on the whole, to be extremely specialist and are followed by the dedicated shooter.

Of them all, Sporting Shooting is the one practised by the vast majority of shooters because it simulates birds normally encountered in the field by the live bird shooter and, in a modified form, is extremely flexible. It can be organised, given the ground and traps, with few problems. Skeet, on the other hand, with its two fixed trap houses, high and low, requires a permanently sited ground.

Sporting Shooting, encompassing as it does, clay targets simulating crossing pigeon, oncoming grouse, high pheasants, bolting rabbits and springing teal, to name a few, can be shot with a standard side-by-side game gun, an over-and-under, semi-auto or pump. The sport was at one time so closely associated with live shooting that only side-by-side game guns were considered suitable. However, times and fashions change and today this discipline may be shot by any of the above specified types of shotgun.

Skeet is nearly always shot with an over-and-under or a semi-auto. Targets are thrown in a straight line from two opposing trap houses and the shooters move in a semi-circle so obtaining a brace of shots at different angles at each of the seven stands. Guns must fit perfectly and be flat shooting; barrel lengths will be about 27-28 inches and the gun will weigh in the region of 7½ to 8½ lb. This is considerably heavier than the standard game gun, but as the shooter may fire 100 plus cartridges he needs to minimise recoil.

LP—D

The going-away disciplines – Down-the-Line, Olympic Trap, Universal Trench and Automatic Ball Trap – demand a different gun approach. These disciplines are all based on live pigeon shooting from traps (illegal in Britain but still practised in a few countries). Just as the bird, when released from its trap flies rapidly away from the shooter, so the clay is ejected away on a rising path from the gun.

To cope with the going-away, rising target the gun must be straight stocked with a comb height on the stock, which will enable the shooter to have a high sighting plane so that the pattern of shot will be printed just above the point of aim, thus ensuring that the target is always in view; if missed, a quick second shot can be taken. Long-barrelled guns, either semi-autos or over-and-unders, are normally used. The top rib will be ventilated to reduce heat and mirage haze; with an over-and-under there is obviously a choice of chokes and today many shooters use half and full. For the single-barrelled semi-auto, whilst chokes of varying degrees can be screwed into, or onto, certain makes of guns, such as the Breda, Winchester and Perrazi, where there is only one choice of choke experienced shooters invariably choose full choke.

FITASC Sporting, whilst similar in concept to English Sporting, is a more refined and testing discipline. A round consists of 25 targets for each shooter with up to 6 members in a squad.

Again, any type of shotgun may be used, though over-and-unders and semi-automatics are the most preferred and the latter has been used to win a world championship.

From all the above it will be seen that the semi-automatic plays an important role in clay shooting, rough shooting, pigeon shooting and wildfowling. It can be used either as a maid-of-all-work or as a highly specialised gun intended for specific target disciplines.

It is also a fact that semi-autos, due to their low perceived recoil, are extremely useful for coaching beginners, for ladies and also for the disabled.

5
Sporting Rifles in the UK

In Britain there are two distinct categories of use for the sporting rifle. Small game and vermin shooting, using either the rim-fire .22 or the much hotter variations of the centre-fire .22, and deer stalking, with centre-fire calibres of .240 and above in England and Wales (Deer Act 1963), and .22 high velocity calibres, such as the .222 Remington, north of the Border for roe deer (Deer Act <Scotland> 1983).

The rim-fire .22 is deservedly popular as a highly useful rifle for controlling rabbits, and vermin such as crows, magpies, grey squirrels and rats. Whilst it is generally agreed by knowledgeable countrymen that hunting them by hounds is by far the most humane method of killing foxes, in some parts of the country no hunt operates and, due to the steady expansion of the fox population, control with a rifle, usually by lamping at night, is essential. Although most operators would prefer to use a centre-fire .22, such as the .22-250 Remington with its 55 grain bullet and 3,800 fps muzzle velocity, the rim-fire Long Rifle high velocity hollow point round at 36 grains and 1,285 fps mv is considered perfectly adequate by some good rifle shots.

It should be made clear that .22 rifles, rim-fire or centre-fire, are never used by legitimate sportsmen against game, other than perhaps the occasional hare. Pheasants, partridges, grouse, etc., duck and geese are the traditional quarry of the shotgunner and should never, under any circumstances, be shot with a rifle, even though the act would not transgress the law.

The semi-auto or auto loading rim-fire .22, though perhaps not always as accurate as the bolt-action rifle, is nevertheless a superb little weapon for dealing with rabbits. Fitted with a good telescopic sight and using 36 grain hollow-point sub-sonic Long Rifle rounds one can pick off bunny after bunny. Solid bullets, coated with grease, although not nearly as effective as the hollow-point, behave like their larger centre-fire cousins, tending to travel straight through the quarry without adequate expenditure of energy. The solid also has the disadvantage of ricocheting if it strikes a stone or branch, whereas the hollow-point is likely to break up or deform under these circumstances.

Quite apart from its very important role in controlling rabbits, rats and winged vermin, the .22 rim-fire provides youngsters, under supervision, with excellent training, particularly if they intend to graduate to deer-stalking and larger calibres.

Fortunately, some common sense has prevailed and it is not proposed that .22 rim-fire, either semi-auto or pump-action, should be placed under Section 5, the prohibited weapon category.

In England and Wales the .22 centre-fire calibres really have only one application today, namely fox control. Since these 'hot' calibres have been banned for shooting the smaller deer, such as roe and muntjac, by the 1963 Deer Act, a role for which they were superbly fitted, they are now largely used by keepers and serious vermin controllers against foxes, usually by lamping at night. It is a curious anomaly that whilst they are considered inadequate against deer south of the Border, in Scotland they are legal for roe and prove highly efficient.

Three basic calibres are used in Britain, the .22 Hornet with a 45 grain bullet and giving 2,690 fps mv, the .222 Remington with a 50 grain bullet, and 3,200 fps mv and the famous .22-250 Remington with a 55 grain bullet and 3,810 fps mv. This last can prove accurate to 325 yards and is certainly sufficiently powerful to put down roe or even fallow, but, as explained above, is illegal in England and Wales for deer stalking.

Deer stalking, coupled with deer control, is now a major and vital sporting activity in Britain yet it has a curiously short history. Red deer stalking on the open hill in Scotland developed as a traditional sport during the middle and latter part of the last century, but it was not until after the Second World War that lowland woodland deer stalking, control and management really started to take off. Roe deer had been, and were still to be, treated almost as vermin to be shot at on pheasant shooting days with light game shot, or driven to shotguns at the end of the shooting season. There was no attempt at management or realisation that these delightful creatures constituted a valuable asset to any estate and had a right to be treated with compassion and respect.

However, many soldiers returning after the War from service in Germany had come to appreciate the high standards of deer management in that country and to realise that we, in Britain, were neglecting our deer population. Through their influence, associated with the stalwart efforts of the British Deer Society and, to some extent, the St Hubert Club, the status of deer was reversed so that, today, they are recognised as a precious countryside resource.

There are six species of deer resident in this country – red, fallow, sika, roe, muntjac and Chinese water deer. Two of these, roe and muntjac, are expanding their range at an astonishing rate. Roe are now found in the entire southern part of England with the exception of Kent and Cornwall, in part of East Anglia and the Midlands, and populate the entire north of England and Scotland. There is little reason to believe that their rate of expansion will be curtailed and soon Wales and most of the Midlands may well be populated by this, the most attractive of deer.

Muntjac, the tiny barking deer from India, standing barely 16 in at the shoulder, escaped from Woburn at the turn of the century and has spread rapidly ever since so that today the whole of East Anglia, the Midlands and much of the South has large populations of this small deer.

Fallow and sika remain fairly static in their populations but red deer in Scotland are causing a great deal of concern as the national herd, according to figures produced by the Red Deer Commission, has reached a total of 220,000, consisting of 83,000 stags, 155,000 hinds and 52,000 calves. Unfortunately, the ratio of stags to hinds has now grown way out of proportion with only 20,000 stags being shot (24%) and 19,000 hinds (12%) and 2,500 calves (5%). Far more hinds need to be shot if correct management is to be exerted for the good of the herd.

Roe now provide woodland stalking on an extensive scale. Many stalkers simply manage tracts of woodland, either to assist estates to control and manage their deer, or for their own benefit, but always with the object of furthering the welfare of the deer. The public know little of the expansion of roe and the damage they can cause to commercial forestry interests, nor do they understand deer stalking.

A great many visitors from abroad, particularly from the Continent, have long recognised the quality of British deer, particularly the roe and sika. The only hindrance to their participation is the requirement that each visitor from abroad must take out a Firearm Certificate, even though he may only be stalking for a day or so. This is normally arranged by a resident who acts as his host, but is an unnecessary and costly piece of bureaucracy which could be dealt with in a more intelligent and simplified fashion.

Whilst by far the majority of deer stalking rifles are centre-fire and bolt-action, a handful of stalkers prefer a sem-auto. In England and Wales, however, the 1963 Deer Act stipulates that the calibre of rifles used must be larger than .240 in and the muzzle energy in excess of 1,700 ft lb. The result is that the most popular calibres used for stalking in Britain are the .243 Winchester, the .270Win,6mm Remington and .308Win. Virtually all these rifles will be bolt-action of one type or another.

Deer stalking is now recognised as a fast expanding sport in its own right and one which, if the deer population in this country is to be correctly managed and cared for, must be given every sensible encouragement.

6
Background to Legislation

The first Act of any serious consequence, as far as the ordinary sportsman, was concerned, was the Firearms Act 1920. This instrument, in effect, laid the foundations for subsequent legislation, though it referred specifically to firearms and excluded from its provisions both smoothbore shotguns, air-guns and their respective ammunition. Basically it provided for a firearm certificate which had to be obtained to possess a rifle or handgun.

There were various exclusions within the Act and it is amusing to note that an officer of the Post Office could apparently carry a firearm in the course of his duties without the need for a firearm certificate.

At that date, 1920, the cost of a firearm certificate was five shillings (25p) and renewal was 2/6d (12½p)

The next Act was the Firearms Act 1937 which simply extended the provisions of the 1920 Act and included references to 'prohibited weapons'. A smoothbore shotgun could be held without a firearm certificate provided the barrel exceeded 20 in, a clause which at a later date was to be increased to 24 in. Certain other provisions were made relating to young persons and their possession and use of firearms and air weapons.

Current legislation is based on the 1968 Firearms Act, an Act which consolidates the Acts of 1937 and 1965, the Air Guns and Shotguns Act 1962, Part V of the Criminal Justice Act 1967, and certain enactments amending the 1937 Act.

Obviously, it would be pointless to cover every provision of that Act; however, I will deal with those which are pertinent to the proposals incorporated in the proposed Firearms (Amendments) Bill 1988 as far as they effect live shooting and clay shooting in this country.

Firstly, anyone who has in his possession or wishes to purchase or acquire a firearm must have a firearm certificate. The same provision applies to the ammunition required for that firearm. There are no exclusions other than smoothbore shotguns with barrels not less than 24 in in length and air weapons which are deemed not to be specially dangerous. Air rifles which fall into this last category require a firearm certificate if they exceed a muzzle energy of 12 ft lbs or in the case of an air pistol 6ft lbs.

As far as ammunition is concerned cartridges containing five or more shot, none of which exceeds .36 in diameter, ammunition for air-guns, rifles and pistols, and blank cartridges, not more than one inch in diameter measured immediately in front of the rim of the cartridge, are all exempt.

A firearm certificate will be granted by a Chief Constable if he is satisfied that the applicant has a good reason to possess a firearm and ammunition and can be permitted to have it in his possession without danger to the public safety or the peace. It will not be granted if the Chief Constable believes the applicant to be of unsound mind, of intemperate habits or for any reason unfitted to be entrusted with such a firearm. Anybody who has been sentenced to any form of custody is also prohibited from possessing a firearm; for life if the sentence was three years or more, and for five years if it was between three months and three years.

It will be noted, then, that there is an implied onus on the applicant to show he has a good reason to possess a firearm. This would normally be for deer stalking and control, vermin control or target shooting under the aegis of a club. The Chief Constable can also vary the conditions on which the firearm certificate is held.

Where shotguns are concerned a different situation applies. The Chief Constable must grant or renew a certificate unless the applicant is prohibited by the Act from possessing a gun or 'cannot be permitted to possess a shotgun without danger to the public safety or the peace.'

In other words, by law the Chief Constable must issue a shotgun certificate unless he can put forward a good reason for witholding it. There is, of course, a right of appeal to quarter sessions in England and Wales, and to the Sheriff Court in Scotland.

A shotgun certificate allows the possession of an unlimited number of guns; it licences the applicant to possess shotguns, whereas a firearm certificate licences the individual weapons and the applicant to possess them.

In the case of a firearm certificate the police exert close control over the movement of privately owned firearms as every sale or movement of a rifle or hand-gun is noted on the certificate and reviewed by the police. Private sales can only take place between individuals who themselves possess firearm certificates authorising the transaction.

Where shotguns are concerned, production of a shotgun certificate is required before an individual can purchase or acquire a shotgun, whether through a dealer or by private acquisition.

Prohibited Weapons

As the law stands at the moment a prohibited weapon is a 'firearm' which is so designed or adapted that, if pressure is applied to the trigger, missiles continue to be discharged until pressure is removed from the trigger or the magazine containing the missiles is empty.' Or 'any weapon of whatever description designed or adapted for the discharge of any noxious liquid, gas or other thing; and any ammunition containing, or designed or adapted to contain, any such noxious thing.'

In simple terms, we are basically dealing with automatic military weapons such as machine guns or flame throwers. Curiously, through inadequate definition in the 1968 Act, portable rocket launchers, bazookas and mortars are not included under Section 5, a loophole which the new Act intends to rectify.

Visitors from Abroad

The past two decades have seen an ever-increasing volume of visitors from abroad to enjoy the superb game shooting available. A substantial industry has developed in Scotland, part of Wales and England to cater for these sportsmen and women. Hotels, estates, game farms and thousands of individuals have geared their economies to sporting visitors from overseas, earning valuable foreign revenue.

Common sense has, till now, prevailed, Section 14 of the 1968 Act noting that 'A person who has been in Great Britain for not more than 30 days in all in the preceding twelve months may have in his possession, or purchase or acquire, a shotgun without holding a Shotgun Certificate.'

Where firearms are concerned, however, visiting deer stalkers from abroad are forced to take out a firearm certificate even though their stay may be for a day or two. This has to be arranged for them by their host and is a cause of unnecessary bureaucracy.

The problem of ensuring that a visitor leaves with the weapon he brought in to the country is not particularly hard to solve. In South Africa, for instance, a country used to thousands of big game hunters from abroad, a temporary firearms permit is issued at the point of entry, noting the weapon, its type and number, and this permit must be given up when the visitor leaves. Without it he is in considerable trouble.

Other clauses which are relevant to the private individual come under Section 11(1). 'A person carrying a firearm or ammunition belonging to another person holding a Certificate under the Act

may, without himself holding such a Certificate, have in his possession that firearm or ammunition under instruction from, and for
the use of, that other person for sporting purposes only.'

However, this does not permit the handler to fire the gun or rifle.

Sub-Section 5 allows a person, not holding a shotgun certificate,
to borrow a shotgun from the occupier of private premises and use
it on those premises in the occupier's presence. This is also a
reasonable clause as is the following sub-section which permits
individuals to use shotguns at 'a time and place approved for shooting at artificial targets by the chief officer of police for the area in
which that place is situated.'

This, then, is the current situation as far as the law is concerned.
Since 1920 strict controls have been exercised over rifles and hand-
guns, whilst shotguns have also been subject to reasonable controls
since 1968. There is not the slightest doubt that the Police Federation have been strongly in favour of tightening up security as far as
shotguns are concerned and would clearly like to see all shotguns
placed on a Part 1 firearm certificate basis. Quite bluntly, the police
believe that there are far too many shotguns in private hands and
they would greatly prefer to see the number reduced. Their argument is that shotguns are increasingly used in crime and the guns
stolen from private homes are likely to be used to commit further
and more serious crimes.

Unfortunately for their case, the facts and figures at once destroy
the argument. Rifles and pistols have been tightly controlled since
1920 and have had to be secured, in the home, in a form of security
cabinet acceptable to the police. Shotguns, on the other hand, have
not required a security provision. One would assume therefore that
far more shotguns than firearms would have been stolen since 1968.

Look again at the *facts* before making any judgement. In 1969
there were 1,299,000 thefts. Of that total there were 384 thefts of
pistols and rifles and 571 shotguns. There were at the time 216,281
firearm certificates and 637,108 shotgun certificates in circulation.

In 1986 there were 2,890,000 thefts. From that well over doubled
figure there was a total of 282 thefts of pistols and rifles and 804
shotguns, but the number of firearm certificate holders had been
reduced to 160,285, whilst shotgun certificate holders had
increased to 840,951.

Reference to Table A, on page 43, clearly indicates that, whilst
thefts overall have steadily and dramatically increased, thefts of
firearms and shotguns have remained remarkably constant.

How many firearms and shotguns are in circulation? Estimates
indicate something in the region of 60,000 pistols and perhaps

42

TABLE A

Year	Total Thefts and Burglaries	Pistols	Thefts of Rifles	Shotguns	No of certificates Firearms	Shotgun
1969	1,299,000	168	184	571	216,281	637,108
1970	1,346,000	130	169	605	–	–
1971	1,414,000	131	154	655	190,649	715,453
1972	1,408,000	126	126	618	–	–
1973	1,352,000	119	123	538	–	–
1974	1,628,000	165	164	608	185,865	766,952
1975	1,743,000	153	141	673	–	–
1976	1,756,000	156	133	666	–	–
1977	2,043,000	166	161	707	–	–
1978	1,959,000	153	132	627	–	–
1979	1,919,000	136	119	551	169,590	782,074
1980	2,047,000	155	109	608	168,047	781,854
1981	2,285,000	205	117	723	164,872	785,225
1982	2,522,000	189	111	716	162,696	780,629
1983	2,474,000	163	111	660	159,804	783,387
1984	2,660,000	164	103	678	160,307	798,352
1985	2,710,000	176	72	722	160,385	819,333
1986	2,890,000	177	105	804	160,285	840,951

100,000 plus rifles, whilst there could be anything between two and three million shotguns.

It is a fact then that shotguns, which are vastly more numerous than firearms, and not subject to their stringent security conditions, are proportionately stolen less frequently than firearms.

The criminal statistics for England and Wales for 1984 are worth examining in some detail. On October 3, 1985, figures were published as they related to offences involving firearms and the Press, in their usual fashion, rose to the bait. The *Daily Mail*, for instance, ran a headline 'GUNLAW TAKES OVER AS CRIME HITS RECORD PEAK', a claim which was hardly borne up by examination of the statistics.

The total number of 'notifiable offences recorded by the police in which firearms were reported to have been used' rose from 7,961 in 1983 to 8,376 in 1984, a rise of 5%. However, it must be carefully noted that this type of offence, whilst it includes homicide and robberies, also covers trivial offences such as the misuse of air- guns. Some 3,417 such cases occurred, often amounting to no more than the breaking of a pane of glass, However, if the damage exceeds £20 a 'crime' is committed.

The next largest grouping of offences is minor injuries caused by air-guns and here there were 2,329 cases, the vast majority caused by children. Whilst bad enough in themselves, petty offences with air-guns can hardly be classified as armed crime.

What of the latter in this period?

In 1984 there were 2,098 robberies in which a firearm was used, representing an increase of about 7% on the 1,957 cases the previous year, but this percentage must be seen in the context of an increase in robberies of all types from 22,119 in 1983 to 24,890 in 1984 in 1984, an increase of 12%. In 1984 firearms were used in 0.4% of all robberies, precisely the rate for 1983 and less than the rate for the preceding decade.

It is worth examining, with care Table B below which provides a breakdown of the 2,098 robberies in which firearms were used. Note that the use of long-barrelled shotguns fell, whilst sawn-off shotguns increased by only six cases over the peak figure of 1982.

Now take a look at Table C. You will see that while the number of cases of homicide by shooting in 1984 was the highest recorded in a decade, shooting is well down the list of favoured means of causing death. The sharp instrument is by far the most used weapon.

A year later in 1985 the number of homicides had fallen to close to the average for the decade, though the number of robberies in which a firearm was used had increased to 2,500, some 60 short of the peak in 1982. The number of recorded burglaries in which a firearm was used was 125, which is 50% higher than the average of 83 for the decade.

Nevertheless, it should be carefully noted that the use of firearms in crime is rare – less than 0.3 per cent of notifiable offences recorded in 1985 involved a firearm. In 1985 the offence group with the highest recorded usage was robbery at 9%; for homicide the rate was 7.3%; for attempted murder and other more serious offences of robbery against the person, 5%; for other less serious offences against the person, 2.3% and for criminal damage over £20,1%. These rates are all similar to those of previous years.

As far as burglary and "other" offences are concerned the recorded usage of firearms was less than two in 10,000 cases.

In 1985 firearms caused injury in about 2,900 notifiable offences and whilst this was 16% more than the previous year, it was nevertheless about 150 lower than the peak year of just over 3,000 in 1979. The number of fatal injuries in 1985 was 45, similar to the average for the decade to that year. However, the number of serious injuries was about 22% higher than in 1984 and nearly 40% higher than the average for the decade. There were about 2,400 slight injuries which was 16% more than in 1984 but about 10% fewer than in the peak year of 1979.

Just under 2,400 thefts and burglaries were recorded in 1985 in which firearms were stolen, a drop of about 10% against the aver-

TABLE B

Offences of robbery recorded by the police in which firearms were reported to have been used by type of weapon

England and Wales								Number of robberies	
Year	Total	Air	Long-weapon	Sawn-off barrelled shotgun	Pistol shotgun	Rifle	Imitation firearm	Supposed firearm	Other firearm
1974	650	69	129	81	260	5	59	40	7
1975	958	96	184	112	370	14	97	75	10
1976	1,076	99	223	183	400	9	89	62	11
1977	1,234	80	257	221	489	18	89	67	12
1978	996	70	181	239	348	6	78	68	6
1979	1,038	58	148	227	386	10	104	82	22
1980	1,149	105	127	181	529	12	113	73	11
1981	1,893	103	262	282	1,001	8	152	67	18
1982	2,560	104	364	372	1,440	10	141	112	17
1983	1,957	80	269	342	1,011	13	120	105	17
1984	2,098	90	216	378	1,106	10	127	149	22

TABLE C

England and Wales

Apparent method	1974	1975	1976	1977	1978	1979	1980	1981	1982	1983	1984
					Number of Offences						
Sharp instrument	146	139	150	135	159	191	158	175	190	151	195
Blunt instrument	59	40	62	65	57	67	61	55	68	68	77
Hitting, Kicking etc.	87	92	81	79	88	82	86	77	70	69	79
Strangulation or asphyxiation	93	69	94	68	79	103	89	87	108	103	92
Shooting	46	43	43	28	35	48	19	32	46	39	63
Explosion	42	9	1	–	2	1	–	3	11	6	6
Burning	18	18	19	12	9	14	95	23	29	19	16
Drowning	5	6	10	8	15	14	14	5	8	8	6
Poison or drugs	16	6	8	6	11	13	9	15	10	8	6
Motor Vehicle	2	7	8	6	4	4	13	13	8	3	4
Other	8	8	9	9	11	8	5	12	5	7	16
Not known	4	6	3	2	1	1	–	2	2	2	3
TOTAL	526	443	488	418	471	546	549	499	555	483	563
					Percentages						
Sharp instrument	28	31	31	32	34	35	29	35	34	31	35
Blunt instrument	11	9	13	16	12	12	11	11	12	14	14
Hitting, Kicking etc.	17	21	17	19	19	15	16	15	13	15	14
Strangulation or asphyxiation	18	16	19	16	17	19	16	17	19	21	16
Shooting	9	10	9	7	7	9	3	6	8	8	11
Explosion	8	2	–	–	–	–	–	1	2	1	1
Burning	3	4	4	3	2	3	17	5	5	4	3
Drowning	5	6	2	2	3	3	3	1	1	2	1
Poison or drugs	3	1	2	1	2	1	2	3	2	2	1
Motor Vehicle	–	2	2	1	1	1	2	3	1	1	1
Other	2	2	2	2	2	1	1	2	1	2	3
Not known	1	1	1	–	–	–	–	–	1	–	–
TOTAL	100	100	100	100	100	100	100	100	100	100	100

age for the decade and of this number some 1,100 – about 45% were air weapons.

Pistols stolen were 15% fewer than the peak of 1981 and shotguns, reported stolen in 722 incidents, remained about the same as 1981. Over the decade there was no discernible trend where shotguns were concerned.

It is interesting to note that whilst there were 1,105 notifiable offences in which a shotgun was used in 1985, there was a total of 1,390 offences involving pistols. This despite the fact that since 1920 pistols have been subject to stringent control and there has been an inexorable tightening of security measures since 1968.

As far as 1986 is concerned the total number of notifiable offences in which weapons were used was 9,363, a considerable reduction on the 1985 figure of 9,742. There were 51 homicides, an increase of six over 1985 but lower than 1984 which had 67. Offences involving criminal damage (usually air weapons) amounted to 4,140, the number of robberies increased from 2,500 to 2,651, but offences of burglary were down from 125 to 96.

Offences in which firearms were reported to have been stolen in 1986 were 2,555, an increase of 155 over 1985 but still well down on the average for the decade. In 1981, for instance, the figure was 2,842 and 3,071 in 1977. There was an increase in the number of shotguns stolen from 722 to 804. This increase is disturbing but hardly a justification for the panic measures now proposed.

It is a fact, a hard, bitter fact, that a criminal can, and will, acquire a weapon, be it shotgun, pistol or rifle, whenever and wherever he chooses. The police are perfectly well aware that there is a pool of unlicenced weapons available for criminal purposes.

When, on a previous occasion similar restrictions to those now being proposed, were considered by the then Home Secretary, Leon Brittan, he said, "we have reviewed the controls on firearms, particularly on shotguns, but have concluded that we should not change the law at present." He continued, "No system of control, no matter how strict, could ever totally prevent a determined criminal acquiring a weapon. As evidence of this, one needs to look no further than the control on Section 1 Firearms (rifles and hand guns). These are generally accepted to be as strict as they reasonably could be, but that has not stopped pistols being used in armed robberies, for example, far more than shotguns."

Hungerford and after

On August 19, 1987 Michael Ryan shot and killed 16 innocent people and wounded another 14, using a Chinese copy of the

Kalashnikov AK47. The story is now part of the sad sweepings of history, but the aftermath of the hysteria whipped up by certain elements of the Press is, predictably, helping to railroad proposals which have clearly not been thought through with clarity or foresight. Obstensibly the Government claims a desire to produce a measured and sensible response but the reality is a hotch-potch of ill-conceived measures which, as usual, will act as a sop to the public conscience without addressing themselves to the problem – the suppression of crime, armed or otherwise.

Hungerford, sadly, was exactly what the Association of Chief Police Officers (ACPO) was waiting for in order to try to pressurise the Government into introducing legislation which would place all categories of shotgun on Section 1 basis. This would then enable them to reduce the number of shotguns legitimately held in private hands by at least half a million, just as they have managed to whittle down Section 1 firearm owners from 240,000 in 1971 to 160,285 at the end of 1986, a steady erosion at the rate of about 4,000 a year.

It was also an ideal opportunity for the Home Office to resurrect the spectre of the firmly, as one hoped, entombed remains of the 1973 Green Paper on firearms, a document whose notorious proposals had been firmly rejected by Parliament.

The circumstances of the Hungerford killings were so bizarre, so out of character for this country, that one would have assumed that common sense would have prevailed and that "panic legislation" would have been overwhelmed by calm deliberation. It was a time when "heat of the moment" views should have been firmly stamped on by Mr Hurd, the Home Secretary and indeed, visiting the scene of the Hungerford massacre on August 24 he appeared to refuse to countenance precipitate action and ruled out emergency legislation before Parliament reassembled in the autumn. He said "I do not think you do these things successfully if you do them in a great hurry. The changes we make should be sensible changes."

It was the lull before the storm.

The next move came at the Conservative Party Conference at Blackpool, October 6-9 when Mr Hurd announced the proposals which were later clarified in the White Paper. The changes proposed were, on the whole, neither sensible, pertinent to the events of Hungerford nor the Bristol killings which took place a few days after the Hungerford tragedy, nor were they likely to ensure the safety of the general public from the irresponsible or criminal use of firearms.

At once Mr Leslie Curtis, Chairman of the Police Federation, expressed disappointment that Mr Hurd had ruled out even tighter

1. *Shotguns have a long and distinguished history. A superb example of a 19th century percussion muzzle-loader.*

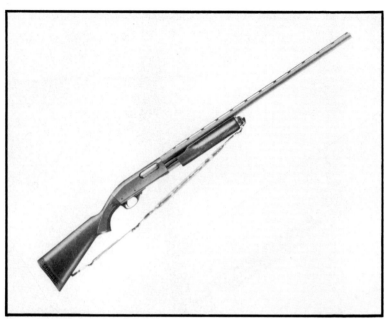

2. *A Remington Model 870 magnum pump-action with 3-inch chambers and 30 inch barrels. This is designed for wildfowling.*

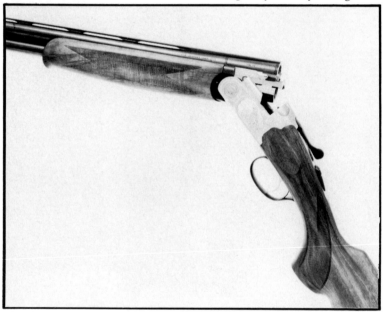

3. *An over-and-under shotgun.*

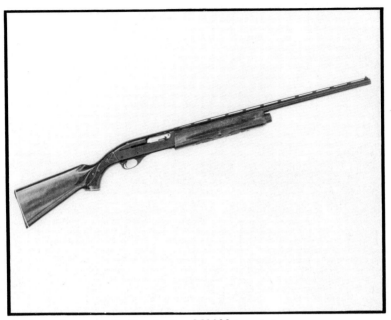

4. A semi-automatic Remington M1100 trap gun.

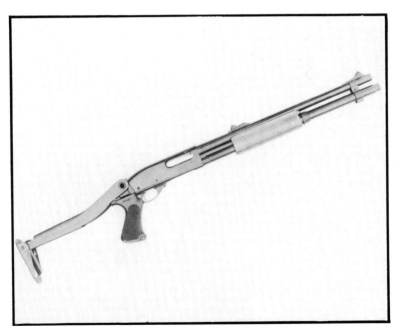

5. A Police Special 21 inch barrelled pump-action with folding stock, magazine extension and rifle sights. Definitely not a sporting gun.

6. *Grouse shooting with a conventional side-by-side shotgun.*

7. *Proposed new legislation could make life more difficult for the solitary rough shooter.*

8. *Clay shooting is a rapidly expanding sport. Restrictions on semi-autos and pump-actions will affect the sport.*

9. *Pigeon shooters find semi-automatics efficient, workmanlike guns.*

10. *A Smith & Wesson 20-bore pump-action shotgun in use – a long-established and perfectly acceptable type of shotgun.*

11. A deer-stalker using a bolt-action rifle, the conventional weapon for nearly all stalkers.

controls over shotguns. He said: "We feel that there are far too many shotguns in the community and far too few controls over them." He went so far as to suggest that all shotguns should be placed on a Section 1 basis.

The Labour Party also quickly revealed their hand where sporting shooting is concerned when Mr Roy Hattersley, the Shadow Home Secretary, announced that Labour would like to see the ownership of shotguns restricted to farmers and target shooters. Opening the Debate in the House on October 26 he said:…"The Opposition accept that the possession and use of firearms is often legitimate and sometimes necessary. Farmers need guns. A man or woman has the right to spend leisure time shooting in competitions or on properly organised target practice…" He went on to say:…"We ought to define far more precisely than is the present practice acceptable reasons for the ownership and use of firearms. Certificates and licences should be issued only to applicants who can demonstrate a specific, explicit and legitimate use. That rule ought to apply, and must apply, to all shotguns. The idea that a shotgun or any number of shotguns may be available to every applicant who passes a perfunctory test is clearly absurd. That is the clear view of the Police Federation which presently carries out that perfunctory test. The check is clearly and unavoidably inadequate. All licences and certificates should be issued for, and thus should legalise the possession of, only one weapon. The dangers of allowing one certificate to legalise the possession of an unlimited number of shotguns are so great and so obvious that to me at least it is astonishing that the system has survived for so long."

The debate made it abundantly clear that many of the Members who chose to speak clearly had little grasp of their subject. Firearms legislation and the complexities of sporting and target shooting are not easily grasped by the layman, however it was clear that emotion and a fundamental inability to differentiate between rifles and shotguns and the legitimate purposes for which they are held ruled the Debate. Thus, inevitably, semi-automatic shotguns were proscribed and equated with Section 5 firearms. The buzz words in the Debate were auto, semi-auto and pump-action and one wonders just how many Members who expressed surprise that the public were allowed access to shotguns and rifles of these types had even a basic understanding of their function.

Sadly, the only reasonable conclusion to be drawn from the October 26 Debate and the attitude of the Police Federation is that, should the Labour Party ever gain power sporting shooting for live quarry would swiftly be banned. Only farmers and "marksmen",

LP—E

required to deal with vermin control, would be in a position to possess guns.

Yet the White Paper itself agrees that..."legislation cannot offer a guarantee against the repetition of the tragic events of Hungerford. It cannot eradicate entirely the possibility of the abuse of legitimately held firearms by an unstable or criminal individual. For that reason the Government must ensure that those firearms which are legitimately held are subject to a degree of control which reduces this risk. The chief duty of the Government is to safeguard the citizen. The Government believes that the extra requirement which it proposes to lay on the shooting community will be accepted by sensible shooters as reasonable."

The White Paper pays lip-service to sportsmen, claiming to recognise that "there is a wide range of legitimate reasons for possessing a firearm. To the farmer or gamekeeper the shotgun is a tool of the trade and is used sensibly and responsibly. Competitive target shooting, rough shooting, game shooting and deer stalking are all legitimate pastimes pursued safely and responsibly by very many people of different backgrounds. Britain has a high and deserved reputation abroad and excellence in some shooting sports. The great majority of firearm and shotgun certificate holders are responsible individuals who pose no threat to public safety. In formulating its proposals the Government has therefore sought to acknowledge and uphold the right of gun users to pursue their work or chosen sport without imposing unnecessary restrictions on them. But balance must not be mistaken for compromise. In many cases the guns concerned are particularly lethal weapons. The Government must ensure that adequate legislation exists to stop them falling into the wrong hands. Those weapons which are especially dangerous and have limited sporting uses should be suitably restricted."

The White Paper and its Proposals

The main features of the Government's proposals in its White Paper published in early December were:

1. To raise certain types of firearm and ammunition into more strictly controlled categories under the 1968 Act. This would involve prohibiting some weapons which now require a firearm or shotgun certificate and requiring a firearm certificate for some weapons which now require only a shotgun certificate.

2. To give the Secretary of State a power to designate certain weapons and ammunition as "prohibited".

3. To prohibit the movement of a weapon into a less strictly controlled category by means of conversion.

4. To require chief officers of police to be satisfied, before granting a shotgun certificate, that the applicant can be permitted to possess a shotgun without danger to the public safety or to the peace.

5. To enable chief officers of police to refuse to issue a shotgun certificate if they are satisfied that the applicant does not have a good reason for possessing a shotgun.

6. To taker powers to require a firearm or shotgun certificate to bear a photograph of the applicant.

7. To require shotguns to be listed on a shotgun certificate and disposals to be notified to the police.

8. To make the purchase of shotgun ammunition subject to production of a valid shotgun certificate.

9. To remove the foreign visitors' exemption from shotgun certificate requirements in section 14 of the 1968 Act and replace it with a tightly drawn permit system.

10. To require that dealers' registrations should be retained for five years after the date of the most recent transaction.

11. To extend the Secretary of State's power to approve rifle clubs for certain purposes to pistol clubs, and limit any such approval to six years.

12. To make provisions for the Royal Ulster Constabulary to exercise greater control over movements of firearms from England, Wales and Scotland to Northern Ireland.

13. To regularize the position of certain museums holding collections.

This then was the nuts and bolts of the Government's proposals which were to be published in the Firearms (Amendments) Bill 1988 on December 17, 1987.

7
For the Defence

Let's get one thing clear from the start. The Firearms (Amendments) Bill contains a number of proposals which are sound, helpful and constructive. To suggest that all the proposals directly violate the interests of the shooting community would be neither helpful nor just and such an attitude, one of unbalanced condemnation, merely plays into the hands of those who would like to see legitimately held sporting guns removed entirely from the public domain.

Perhaps the most significant factor, the one which at once betrays the Government's almost subconscious appreciation of the weakness of their proposals is that, having stated that it has 'consulted widely on its proposals' it has signally failed to take counsel from, or listen to, those who have the experience, the knowledge and background to what is, after all, a complex and momentous subject. To seek comment after proposals have been published, in the knowledge that legislation is to be hurried through Parliament and that any constructive criticism will only take place in the two Houses is at best cynical, at worst devious.

Logic and sheer commonsense would have suggested consultations with the British Association for Shooting & Conservation, the British Shooting Sports Council, the British Deer Society and the British Field Sports Society. As Christopher Brunker, Christie's firearms expert, so succinctly points out in Chapter 9 : 'Firearms and their control are complex matters. Lack of expertise in relation to them is not confined to government, but those entrusted with power have a duty to use it wisely. This they cannot hope to do if they do not grasp the fundamentals. There is a clear need for a permanent, statutory, expert body to advise on firearms law, but the Home Office has consistently resisted this idea.'

The BASC is Britain's largest organisation devoted solely to promoting the interests of sporting shooters allied to the concept of practical conservation. With a membership approaching 100,000, a full-time staff of 45 operating from its rapidly expanding headquarters in North Wales, BASC has a right to be heard and its views given mature and considered scrutiny. That this has not happened is yet another indication of the Government's unwillingness to listen to the voice of reason – or is it simply, and far more likely, that the Government is unwilling to be seen to pay attention to the 'gun lobby' for fear it may appear biased. Yet to listen to advice based on experience is not to lose face. It is an attitude which comes with maturity.

As usual, BASC came under fire from a small but important section of its members who could not understand why, apparently, the Association was dragging its feet. Action, they demanded, something must be done! What that 'something' was nobody seemed to have a clear idea. They failed to appreciate that until the White Paper had been published and the Government's intentions spelt out little of a constructive nature could be done. Speculation could so easily lead to egg on the face.

Once the White Paper had been published the BASC Firearms Department, led by Brian Hughes, swung into action. The result was a paper which examined, word by word, detail by detail, the Government proposals.

There are 48 sections in the paper, nearly all of which are worth printing with the BASC's comments. Where I have thought it pertinent I have included my own comments in italic. The White Paper proposals are set in bold type and the BASC replies in ordinary face.

1. Preamble to the conclusions set out below

2. The Government is concerned to accomodate the needs and interests of the legitimate shooting community in so far as this does not compromise the primary concern of ensuring that firearms controls give adequate and effective protection to the community at large.

The BASC is pleased that this statement has been made, entirely supports its sentiments and will continue working to achieve this objective.

3. But legislation cannot offer a guarantee against a repetition of the tragic events at Hungerford. It cannot eradicate entirely the possibility of the abuse of legitimately held firearms by an unstable or criminal individual.

The BASC's long-held view is in complete agreement with this statement and emphasises the necessity for issuing shotgun and firearm certificates only to responsible people.

4. The proposals outlined in this White Paper mark a considered

and significant shift in the balance of controls between safeguarding the public at large and protecting the interests of the legitimate shooting community.

The Government's own actions and calendar indicate that these proposals are not 'considered'. Firstly, there was no prior consultation with representative shooting organisations and, secondly, the time span between the publication of the White Paper (December 2, 1987) and the Bill (December 17, 1987) did not allow for wide discussion and subsequent amendment of the proposals. It is an area of legal and technical complexity which demanded a more realistic timescale so that proper consultation could be entered into to ensure the full democratic process and the achievement of mutually desired objectives.

Paragraphs 5-13 cover the present law and paragraph 14 outlines the proposals.

15. The strict controls which apply to prohibited weapons under Section 5 of the Act will be extended to cover a number of additional types of firearms:
– self-loading and pump-action rifles (other than those chambered for .22 rim-fire) and carbines.
– burst fire weapons (rifles, carbines and pistols).
– self-loading or pump-action short barrelled smooth bore guns. – portable rocket launchers, bazookas and mortars.

These proposals will prohibit a number of weapon types which clearly have no role in the sporting field, but they will also catch up a number of sporting and target centre-fire rifles. The BASC feels that the prohibiting of self-loading and pump-action sporting rifles is unnecessary as they are made with a limited magazine capacity (usually 4 or 5) and have no greater fire-power capacity than the average bolt-action sporting rifle. These rifles are often used by persons who suffer from recoil. A clear definition of 'portable rocket launchers' is required so as not to exclude flares used by yachtsmen and wildfowlers for safety reasons.

The BASC supports the BSSC proposal that, as an alternative to banning all semi-automatic and pump-action rifles (other than .22 rim-fire), there should be a schedule of approved rifles of this type to include both target and sporting rifles.

16. Self-loading rifles (of which Kalashnikovs are one example)

55

are designed primarily for military use, and have a rate of fire and a magazine which makes them especially lethal. Many are adaptations or conversions of weapons capable of fully automatic fire, and in some cases they can be converted back to their fully automatic capability relatively simply. These weapons are used in "practice shooting", and in a few Service rifle competitions in which some civilians participate. Perhaps 5% of firearms certificate holders in Great Britain (out of a total of 200,000) own such weapons. They are particularly lethal and dangerous. The Government feels that despite their limited sporting uses they should be banned.

The Gun Trade Association Ltd. estimates that there are some 10,000 mainly target, but a few sporting, rifles in this category currently held in lawful ownership. The BASC proposes action as per 15 above.

17.   Burst fire weapons discharge a limited number of missiles (usually 3 or 5) in response to a single pressure on the trigger. There are no legitimate sporting or recreational uses for these weapons outside the military arena. Some types of short-barrelled smooth bore guns do have a recognised use (examples include rook guns, Very pistols and muzzle loaders) and, having listened to representations, the Government has no wish to prohibit these. The provision therefore relates only to repeating weapons of this sort and is intended primarily to catch military style shotguns which have a shorter overall length than conventional shotguns and a much greater firing capacity. Portable rocket launchers, bazookas and mortars do not at present fall within the prohibited category by reason of inadequate definition in the 1968 Act. They are lethal weapons and this gap must be stopped.

The BASC notes with approval that the Government has no wish to prohibit certain weapons which could have been caught up by the original proposal as stated by the Home Secretary on September 22.

18.   In addition it is intended to put beyond doubt that devices known as stun guns are prohibited weapons for the purposes of Section 5 of the 1968 Act.

The BASC recognises the potential hazard that a weapon which passes an electric shock through the victim creates. This could be extremely dangerous.

19. New weapons are being developed all the time, and new types of repeating firearms could appear on the market. The Government therefore proposes to intruduce a reserve Order-making power enabling the Secretary of State to designate any firearm or shotgun as a prohibited weapon for the purposes of Section 5 of the Act, if it appears to be especially dangerous; and similarly ammunition.

This section effectively puts the designation of any firearm or shotgun and ammunition solely at the discretion of the Secretary of State at the Home Office and insidiously confers powers upon him or her to amend designations without any consultation. It in effect gives the Secretary of State the power to eliminate whole classes of shooting sports, their firearms or ammunition. BASC totally opposes this proposal as it stands, though recognises that clearly the status of new weapons needs to be reviewed. This should be done through consultation with a statutory Expert Advisory Committee and approved by Parliament in the normal democratic process.

This is without question a totally unacceptable proposal giving, as it does, the Secretary of State powers which go way beyond the democratic process.

20. It is unsatisfactory that the present law has been held to allow weapons to be converted from one classification to another. In particular the Government is concerned about the growing trade in military and other firearms converted from one classification to another. In many cases these can be restored to their original condition without the need for any professional skills. This is particularly worrying in the case of fully automatic weapons (machine-guns) converted to single shot weapons. The present situation, in which considerable numbers of weapons are converted and the standard of conversion ranges widely, leads to uncertainty about the legal status of many of these weapons. This in turn complicates the work of the police in enforcing firearms control. The Government therefore thinks it is desirable to introduce greater clarity in this area. In future any firearm which has been deactivated or converted from a high classification to a lower one will retain its original, high classification.

The Government is concerned about the growing trade in military and other firearms converted from one classification to another, particularly fully-automatic weapons (machine-guns) coverted to the self-loading mode. Many firearms have been converted to shotguns but this is a grey area of law and there are conflicting court judgements. The technical and legal complexity requires governmental consultation with a statutory Expert Advisory Committee.

21.   Section 1 controls now apply to most rifles and handguns. The Government proposes to bring all pump-action and self-loading shotguns of normal length (with a barrel of 24 inches or over) under Section 1 controls. These types of weapons are used for legitimate sporting purposes, and also for vermin control. There are relatively few instances in which a traditional shotgun will not serve as well as a pump-action or self-loading shotgun. In view of the higher rate of fire of shotguns of this kind, and the availability in most cases of an alternative weapon (i.e. a traditional shotgun), it is reasonable that they should come under Section 1 controls. Those who want to hold such weapons will have to satisfy the police that they have a good reason for wishing to do so. If manufacturers were able to make in future a pump-action or self-loading shotgun with a capacity of only 3 shots and which was not convertible, it might be regarded as more acceptable for sporting purposes.

The BASC considers this a totally unnecessary proposal. No evidence has been produced to link these weapons in any particular way to the commission of crime. There are estimated to be 200, 000 of these shotguns currently in circulation and they have been used legitimately since the turn of the century. World-wide, these two types of shotgun taken together are the most numerous in use for sporting purposes. The BASC is vehemently opposed to this unjustified proposal.

The Government's advisors have clearly undertaken no research or even begun to understand the use and requirement for semi-automatic shotguns and pump-actions. Are they even aware that the short-recoil Browning semi-automatic with a capacity for two shots only has been in circulation for many years, although no longer available? There is no just case or reason for these types of shotgun to be placed on a Section 1 firearms basis.

22.   There is a marked difference in the level of controls exercised over Section 1 firearms and shotguns under Section 2 of the 1968 Act. In relation to the former a chief officer of police must be satisfied that a number of criteria are fulfilled before granting a certificate. But under present legislation, the chief of police must grant a shotgun certificate unless he has reason to believe that the applicant is prohibited by the Act (e.g. by reason of a previous conviction)

from possessing a shotgun, so that such possession by the applicant will endanger the public safety or the peace. The certificate enables the holder to purchase and possess unlimited and unlisted numbers of shotguns, and there is no obligation on him to store his weapons securely when he is not using them. The Government believes that this control is too weak.

The BASC does not believe that current controls are too weak. In theory a shotgun certificate does allow the purchase of an unlimited number of shotguns but, in practice, this is not the case. The great majority of sportsmen have only sufficient guns for their needs and their pocket. This is rarely more than one or two weapons. Statistics already exist which show that firearm and shotgun thefts have been held at a remarkably constant level, whereas over the same period serious and armed crime has more than doubled. Under the current voluntary security system shotguns are stolen less frequently than other firearms which are more tightly controlled and secured. The BASC believes that the present legislation is adequate and no reform is justified.

23. Although most shotgun owners probably already keep their guns safely, there is no legal requirement to this effect. The Government considers that it is now time to bring shotgun security into line with that for Section 1 firearms. This means that shotgun owners will be under a statutory obligation to keep their shotguns in a secure place when not in actual use. (Guidance will make clear that actual use is to include transportation to and from a place of use and/or for purposes of repair). There were over 800 incidents last year (1986) in which shotguns were reported to have been stolen (including 537 thefts from residential properties). Some of these weapons may later be used in the commission of further crimes. Shotguns are extremely dangerous weapons if misused and all reasonable measures should be taken to prevent them falling into criminal hands.

The BASC questions why it is now thought necessary to alter the security status on shotguns since their safe-keeping has not deteriorated since 1969. If the Government arbitrarily imposes statutory shotgun security the BASC is pleased to note that they will 'make clear that actual use is to include transportation to and from a place of use and/or for the purposes of repair'. The BASC also urges that the onus of maintaining their security must fall on the user and not left to the vague discretion of the chief officers of police for arbitrary implementation.

Note that under the published Bill security requirements have not been mentioned. These will however appear in the published rules.

24.   The Government proposes that the balance of the control be shifted by requiring the chief officer of police to be satisfied that the applicant can be permitted to possess a shotgun without danger to the public safety or the peace. This will give the chief officer discretion to satisfy himself, by means of home inspections, that shotguns are being stored securely. The chief officer must have the power to refuse or revoke a certificate if such security is inadequate, as is now the position in respect of Section 1 firearms.

The BASC does not believe that this shift in emphasis is necessary. These specific proposals will give the police additional arbitrary and unnecessary powers. It is questionable whether a right of entry exists just now, since the only specific rights of entry exist under sections 46 and 49 of the 1968 Act (these relate to suspected offences and arms dealing). It should be recognised that, with 908,000 current shotgun certificate holders in Great Britain, a large number of police officers inexperienced in the firearms legislation will have to become involved. This factor, in conjunction with a doubtful right of entry, will lead to direct confrontation with one of the most law-abiding sections of the public.

The BASC suggests that the present extremely successful voluntary safe-keeping of shotguns be enhanced by both education and the continued cooperation between the police and the BASC.

25.   There is concern that shotguns are being acquired for reasons which the Government would regard as unacceptable, including self-defence. The chief officer will in future be able to refuse to issue or renew a shotgun certificate where he is satisfied that the applicant does not have a good reason for having a shotgun in his possession or for purchasing or acquiring a shotgun. It is not intended to impose an obligation on all applicants in every circumstance to establish positively the existence of a good reason, since in the majority of cases this will be readily apparent. But the police should be able to look further into an application which they suspect has no good reason behind it. Guidance will be issued to the police on how the new power is to be exercised, perhaps with some reinforcement of this as part of the legislation, and on the sorts of case in which further enquiries may be necessary.

BASC agrees that in the majority of cases it will be comparatively easy to establish good reason, but experience shows that some police officers may use this as a further method to reduce the number of shotgun certificates granted. Establishing good reason could lead to the requirement for written proof, to the inspection of land to assess its suitability and, in turn, to territorial conditions. Bearing in mind the well known and legitimate universal use of shotguns, the establishment of a particular good reason must be a bureaucratic nonsense, leading once again to confrontation.

Under current legislation the police can invoke the 'danger to the public safety' and the 'peace' provision in the case of doubtful applicants.

26. The Government intends that shotguns be listed by serial number, or by a description where there is no such number, on a shotgun certificate. Anyone applying for a shotgun certificate will be obliged to provide the police with these details so that they can be recorded on the certificate. In addition, where a shotgun is sold or otherwise transferred, the transferor will be obliged to endorse the details on the recipient's certificate and to notify the police of the transaction; likewise the recipient will also be required to notify the police. It is remarkable that the police at present have so little information either about individual's weapons or about the number of shotguns legally held. The Government believes that we must begin to fill this void. Such recordings would allow for the eventual introduction of a central guns register if, on further examination, this seemed desirable.

The police and the Home Office have consistently refused to co-operate with proper research proposals. The BASC view this paragraph with grave concern, on five points. Firstly, the current estimate of 3 million shotguns could, if central registration were to be considered, require the establishment of a national administrative centre roughly one quarter the size of the DLVC in Swansea, in addition to the 52 constabulary offices.

Secondly, there will inevitably be confusion since shotgun and firearm serial numbers are not unique. Some manufacturers produce different models which have identical numbers.

Thirdly, to be effective the records would not only have to be accurately recorded but also meticulously maintained.

Fourthly, this data base has to be established on information voluntarily provided by the owners. Will this be acceptable to the police? If not satisfied, will the police then invoke section 49 of the Firearms Act and seek entry to houses on a search warrant?

Finally, this represents a major shift in police manpower from detection and prevention of crime to purely bureaucratic work.

27. There will continue to be an appeal against any refusal of a shotgun certificate.

No action required.

28. Irrelevant.

29. The Government has considered carefully whether it would be right to intruduce more stringent controls over the storage of ammunition in the home, but has concluded that the disadvantages of this approach outweigh any potential benefits. Although there is clearly some risk inherent in the storage of ammunition at home, there are a number of serious obstacles to compulsory storage at gun clubs. Many clubs do not have secure facilities for storage of weapons or ammunition, and many serious competitive shooters load their own ammunition at home for reasons of economy. It is quite common for shooters to belong to several different clubs and shoot at a number of ranges, and it would be inconvenient and uneconomical for them to store ammunition at each of these premises or to buy a new supply each time they shoot. Storage at clubs is also clearly impractical for those who own firearms for vermin control or game shooting. Above all, the Government feels that such an approach would be irresponsible in providing large and readily identifiable stores of ammunition which might attract the criminal or terrorist.

The BASC agrees with this conclusion.

30. At present the only control on shotgun ammunition is that it may not be sold to, or purchased by, persons under 17. The fact that it may be purchased by a person who does not possess a shotgun certificate makes easier the unauthorised use of shotguns. However, the imposition of full certificate control on the purchase and possession of all shotgun ammunition similar to that relating to Section 1 control would not be feasible in view of the vast numbers of transactions involved. It would tie up a lot of police time, have serious consequences for many traders (particularly in rural areas), and cause considerable inconvenience to shotgun users. A lesser degree of control would avoid these drawbacks while still achieving a worthwhile improvement in security. The Government therefore proposes that anyone seeking to purchase shotgun ammunition should be required

to produce either a valid certificate or a written authority from a certificate holder, together with that certificate, in order to do so. In addition, the more lethal types of shotgun cartridge will be brought under full Section 1 certificate control.

The BASC does not object to the general provision of having to produce a certificate to purchase ammunition, though recognises that bulk purchases from main suppliers may be complicated.

31. The Government intends to introduce revised arrangements for visitors to this country who have been resident here for not more than 30 days in the previous 12 months and who wish to possess or purchase firearms or shotguns and ammunition. At present such persons may purchase or possess any number of shotguns without holding a shotgun certificate. This represents a serious gap in the law which the Government intends to close. Any visitor who wishes to bring a shotgun to this country for sporting purposes will in future need to apply for a visitor's shotgun permit through a sponsoring resident here. For those coming to purchase a shotgun for export purposes only, and not for use, a permit will not be required, but it will be an offence for a visitor to dispose of a shotgun purchased here other than to a registered firearms dealer. Visitors wishing to bring firearms into this country will also be required to obtain a permit through a sponsoring resident here. The permit will not authorise the purchase of firearms.

The Government has not demonstrated a problem in this area, but believes that section 14 of the 1968 Act is open to abuse. Once again, therefore, this represents an unnecessary administrative burden, which the BASC feels bound to emphasise.

33. These provisions will ensure that effective control is maintained over visitors coming to this country to use firearms or to use and purchase shotguns. They will result in the minimum necessary inconvenience to visiting marksmen and sportsmen, and should have no effect on the domestic gun trade.

It is quite obvious that sections 32 and 33 imply that there will be an adverse effect on the domestic gun trade. They already prohibit the purchase of firearms and the BASC urges the Government to include the purchase and export of firearms by visitors into these provisions.

34.   The Government proposes to make a number of changes relating to authorised firearms dealers. In future the status of a firearms dealer will be confined to those who can establish that dealing in firearms is a substantial commercial or business activity. This will help to ensure that only legitimate dealers receive authorisation, and will remove the temptation for firearms enthusiasts to register as dealers simply as a convenient way to pursue their hobby and to collect larger numbers of weapons than may be held by an ordinary certificate holder. In addition, the validity of the period of registration of firearms dealers will be extended from one to three years. This will reduce the burden on the police without any loss of control, since they have the power of entry to dealers' premises which may be exercised at any time.

An unknown number, probably a few, small, part-time registered firearms dealers and those using RFD certificates as a means of collecting firearms may well be affected by this. To the best of our knowledge no evidence has been brought forward showing a problem in this area.

35.   Under Section 9 of the 1968 Act carriers of firearms and ammunition and warehousemen are exempt from normal controls, and are not required to have regard to the security in transit or temporary storage of the goods they are handling. This provision is mainly aimed at exempting from the rigours of controls persons who may possess firearms on an occasional and temporary basis. However the fact that they are not obliged to have regard to the safekeeping of weapons and ammunition in their possession poses a potential security risk which the Government finds unacceptable. We therefore propose to introduce a requirement to ensure the security of firearms or ammunition transported, despatched or collected in Britain.

As yet details are not known relating to this provision and consequently the bureaucratic and practical implications (such as the use of special vehicles for transportation, the employment of specially trained or certificated staff and the impact that this will have on any sale, purchase or repair of a weapon) are unknown. It is anticipated, though, that this provision will make any weapon sale, purchase or repair slower, more costly and difficult.

The published Bill calls for 'reasonable precautions for the safe custody of any firearm or ammunition'. Presumably this will be spelt out in the Rules.

36. All dealers are required to maintain detailed records of their transactions in firearms registers. These help the police to maintain the controls and, in particular, to trace illegally held firearms. The Government therefore intends to add a new requirement for dealers to retain their register for a minimum period of five years after the date of the last entry. Where a firearms dealer ceases to trade for whatever reason he will be required to surrender the register to the police.

The BASC sees no fault with these sensible provisions.

36. The Government will take this opportunity to amend section 6 of the 1968 Act in order to tighten the controls over the carriage of firearms to Northern Ireland. This will enable the Royal Ulster Constabulary to exercise greater control over movements of firearms and ammunition from England, Scotland and Wales to Northern Ireland, and so lessen the likelihood of their falling into the hands of terrorists.

Until details are published the BASC can make no comment.

38. Concern has been expressed over mail order sales and advertising of firearms. The Government has considered this issue carefully, but has decided that any blanket prohibition would represent an unreasonable restriction on trade. Sales of firearms by mail order are subject to the same control as those over the counter and there is no evidence that such sales are being used to evade the law. The Government recognises, however, the concern about the nature of some advertisements and this is being pursued with the Advertising Standards Authority.

The BASC acknowledges the fact that there is to be no direct intervention on mail order. However paragraph 35 (dealing with the transportation of firearms and ammunition) could impinge on the current status of mail order. The BASC recognises that all advertising, including firearms advertising, should conform to ASA standards.

39. Under section 11 of the 1968 Act members of rifle clubs, miniature rifle clubs and cadet corps approved by the Secretary of State may have club firearms and ammunition in their possession without a firearm certificate when engaged as a member of the club or corps for drill or target practice. The main aim of this exemption is to provide for novices of the sport and those who only participate occasionally or who for some other reason do not wish to possess a weapon of their own. In such cases a certificate is issued, free of charge, to the club secretary. Clubs which do not seek the approval of the Secretary of State are not accorded this privilege, and their members must all have their own firearm certificates.

40.   The Government is keen to improve the approval scheme and place it on a new statutory footing. The Secretary of State will therefore be given a specific power to approve both rifle and pistol clubs. Clubs will have to fulfil a number of criteria in order to qualify and approval will be renewable on a six yearly basis. They will have to be properly constituted, have access to a firing range approved by the Secretary of State for Defence, and be run by fit and proper persons. A fee will be introduced for approval and renewal to reflect the adminstrative costs involved.

The BASC will keep a careful watch on this proposal to ensure no new unnecessary restrictions are placed on affiliated bodies.

41.   A provision for raising to life imprisonment the maximum penalty for carrying a firearm in crime has already been included in the Criminal Justice Bill... There is widespread public concern about the rapid growth in crimes involving firearms and this provision reflects the gravity with which the Government views this offence. In addition the maximum penalty for possessing a shotgun without a certificate is being raised to bring it into line with the same offence in respect of firearms (on indictment, three years' imprisonment, or a fine, or both).

The BASC finds this self-explanatory and acceptable.

43.   The Government has considered and decided against a number of other ways in which the controls might be strengthened. The imposition of arbitrary limits on the number of weapons which an individual may possess, or a prohibition on the possession of more than one weapon of each calibre, whilst superficially attractive, would have little significant benefit in terms of control. Such a policy would be against the interests of the genuine shooter, since competitive target shooting often requires the possession of several weapons, some of which may be of the same type or calibre. The same is true, though perhaps to a lesser extent, of sporting guns. In such circumstances the Government feels it is best left to the police,

drawing on guidance, to decide whether an application for a further firearm is supported by a good reason for possessing it. This in itself represents a control on the accumulation of weapons.

The BASC welcomes the statements that the Government does not wish to impose arbitrary limits on the number of weapons in possession, or the possession of more than one weapon of each calibre by an individual. However, by vesting in the police the power to be satisfied as to good reason for the possession of further firearms the Government is providing them with further arbitrary and interpretative powers.

This section clearly provides the police with the power to turn down applications for further shotguns or rifles, on their terms, and is likely to lead to considerable friction.

44. The Government has looked in detail at the form and content of firearm and shotgun certificates and the procedures for their issue. It is exploring the scope for using photographs as part of the certification process and for this reason intends to take powers under the 1968 Act to require an application for a shotgun or firearm certificate to be accompanied by two photographs of the applicant. The Government also intends to extend the current requirement for an application for a shotgun certificate to be countersigned by a person of good character to cover firearm certificate application as well. The Government is not attracted at this stage to the option of seeking medical references from qualified practitioners in support of applications for firearms or shotgun certificates. It has been argued that these would provide a judgement as to the applicant's mental state and psychological fitness to possess a firearm. But reference to an applicant's medical record would provide no guarantee against the issue of a certificate to an unsuitable person; such a system would constitute a significant administrative burden; and difficulties might arise over the issue of medical confidentiality.

The BASC is not averse to the concept of photographs on certificates. They applaud the Government's views on medical records and agree with its conclusions. However, the concept of a signature on a shotgun certificate application was rejected by the ACPO/ Home Office Working Party Report (1984) on the grounds that 'many forces make no enquiries at all about counter-signatories and the requirement seems to serve little useful purpose'. The BASC, therefore, sees no value in having a counter-signature on a shotgun certificate application, let alone on a firearms certificate application. It is their experience that this requirement is socially divisive, acting as a major restraint on certain social classes who have little personal or professional access to those persons whose positions or professions are defined on the form.

45. The Government has already announced its intention of holding a firearms amnesty. This will enable illegally held firearms and shotguns, and those whose owners no longer wish to keep them, to be handed in to the police. The Government has no illusions that an amnesty will remove all illegally held firearms from circulation. But it is sensible to provide an opportunity to reduce the numbers available to prevent them falling into criminal hands. Surrender to the police will ensure that they do not re-enter the market. Previous amnesties have yielded substantial amounts of both guns and ammunition. The amnesty will be timed to coincide with the introduction of the new controls so that owners of weapons which can no longer be held as a result of changes in the law will be able to take advantage of its provisions.

The BASC agrees with this provision but feels that permitting registered firearms dealers to receive such weapons and ammunition would increase the effectiveness of such a measure. Many people would feel more 'comfortable' surrendering weapons to the trade rather than to a police station. Where a weapon or rare ammunition of some value is lawfully owned and surrendered, provision must be made for the owner to realise its value.

46. The Government's proposals have resource implications for both the police and central government. Where apppropriate these will be recovered through the fees charged for shotgun and firearm certificates. In future certificate fees will be reviewed every three years to ensure that they continue to cover the full costs of administration.

The new bureaucratic structure which the Government is imposing on shotgun certification is bound to incur increased costs. Given that all measures contained within the White Paper are aimed towards increased public safety, it could be considered unfair that all costs will inevitably be borne by shotgun certificate holders.

This is simply a blank cheque to enable a Government to increase fees at their own discretion, and for whatever reason they choose, with the ever ready excuse that the full costs of administration must be covered.

47. The Government has also looked carefully at the question of compensation for those people who now own weapons which will become prohibited. We have concluded that as a matter of principle it is undesirable and unjust to require the taxpayer at large to pay for the removal from the public domain of weapons which are an acknowledged threat to life. Although there will be no market for prohibited weapons in this country, authorised dealers will still be able to export them abroad, and owners will be able to recover some of the value in this way. Where they choose not to do so, facilities will be provided for them to be handed in to the police in the course of the forthcoming firearms amnesty.

A basic premise of the White Paper has been that, if good reason can be shown, the possession and use of firearms and shotguns is positively endorsed. However, due to some weapons being an 'acknowledged threat to life', they will now be made illegal. The Government's own endorsement of weapons and their use is contradicted by this exclusion of some categories, and this contradiction runs into pure hypocrisy when it states that, although a threat to life here, they can be exported. Would they not also pose a 'threat to life' overseas? The weapons in question would become virtually valueless in this country due to the measures contained in this Paper and, if done in the interests of public safety, then compensation must be made.

As a matter of principle it can be argued with equal conviction and force that it is undesirable and unjust to remove from the taxpayer weapons formally legally held without some form of compensation. This is arbitrary, unreasonable and smacks of the attitude of a police state.

48. There is no merit in bureaucratic controls for their own sake. The Government has consulted widely on its proposals, which will be closely scrutinised by both Houses of Parliament. The subject is highly technical and to some extent controversial. The Government has no wish to impose onerous additional restrictions on the legitimate shooting community where they will serve no effective purpose. But the Government considers that the proposals laid out in the White Paper represent a well-weighed package which measures the essential issues against the fundamental need to improve the security of the community as a whole.

Throughout this document the BASC has highlighted many areas where bureaucratic control is proposed, control which will not 'improve the security of the community' but which will 'impose onerous additional restrictions on the legitimate shooting community'. The Government recognises the highly technical nature of the subject but makes no reference to the highly desirable establishment of a statutory Expert Advisory Committee. Despite stating that it has 'consulted widely on its proposals', the Government has sought comment for its proposals only after their publication.

8
Defence Pursued

The Firearms (Amendment) Bill breaks down into four principal areas of contention as far as the ordinary sporting shooter is concerned. The first of these is the proposal to transfer semi-auto and pump-action shotguns to Section 1 category, thus placing them on a par with rifles and pistols.

Semi-autos and pump-action shotguns

It has already been clearly demonstrated that both these types of shotgun have a legitimate role to play in the live shooting scene; semi-autos date back to 1902 and pump-actions even earlier to around 1882; taken together these two types of shotgun by far command the greatest number of sales throughout the world. It can, therefore, be argued with force and logic that this situation would hardly have arisen had there been any particular and inherent danger in their ownership or use.

There are no hard facts or figures but as pump-action and semi-autos have been used by sporting shooters in Britain since the early part of this century, it is believed that there are at the very least 200,000 sporting guns of these two types in circulation.

As far as crime is concerned it would be very interesting to know just how many semi-autos and pump-actions have been used in crime compared to "conventional" sawn-off side-by-sides. The latter weapon is the favoured tool of the armed criminal as the barrel can be shortened to within a few inches of the breech and the stock hacked back so that, in effect, it becomes a double-barrelled pistol with an overall length of about 15 in. Such a gun can easily be concealed under a raincoat.

However, the barrel of the sporting semi-auto cannot be shortened beyond the actuating mechanism and it would be extremely difficult to shorten a pump or semi-auto to achieve an overall length of less than 25 in.

The White Paper, in its proposal to transfer semi-autos and pump-actions to Section 1 category weapons notes that: "If manufacturers were able to make in future a pump-action or self-loading shotgun with a capacity of only 3 shots and which was not convertible, it might be regarded as more acceptable for sporting purposes". Chris Cradock, the well-known firearms expert and journalist, believes that it is possible to design magazine tubes which have an inside permanently fixed annular ring, brazed or welded in position, which would make it impossible to convert such a magazine into one to take more than one cartridge.

There are also, of course, a considerable number of Browning 2-shot semi-autos in circulation and it will be interesting to see how they fare under the Bill. They are on par with "conventional" shotguns, as the White Paper chooses to call them, as far as firepower is concerned, yet still come into the semi-auto category.

Who uses these guns? Fairly cheap, efficient and treated as working guns, semi-autos in particular tend to be owned by the less well-off members of the shooting community. They are widely used for rough shooting, wildfowling and vermin destruction and are popular with clay pigeon shooters. Due to their perceived low recoil they are used a great deal for coaching and by those who suffer from recoil such as women and disabled shooters.

As far as semi-autos and pump-action shotguns used for sporting and clay shooting are concerned there is every logical reason why they should remain in Section 2. The sheer logistics of transfering them to Section 1 category is mind-boggling.

If one assumes one of these types of gun per person (say 200,000) this would effectively mean a virtual doubling of the number of firearm certificate holders, with all the attendant work involved, not to mention the innumerable petty incidents and dramas arising from occasions where the police might choose to find reasons why guns should not be transferred and certificates refused. A cynic could suggest that the police might use the opportunity to reduce the number of these guns legitimately held!

Assuming, also, that new security provisions are made which would entail *all* shotguns being held in a secure place there would seem to be neither point nor logic in transferring them to a Section 1 category – unless the move is simply to provide an excuse for reducing their numbers.

Without a shadow of doubt the case for retaining sporting semi-autos and pump-action shotguns in Section 2 category is overwhelming and one is inevitably lead to the conclusion that the proposal to shift them to the Section 1 category is a calculated move designed to reduce their numbers at present legitimately held in private hands.

Security

Security for shotguns is surely a matter of commonsense and the onus of providing a system of security should devolve upon the owner of a gun(s) rather than be made a statutory obligation with all its attendant ills revolving around interpretation from one police force to another. If a gun is stolen then the owner should be made responsible and liable to prosecution.

The fact of the matter is that the police themselves do not require or desire a statutory security provison. At the first meeting of the Working Party on Firearms Fees and Shotgun Security Mr Oxford, representing the Association of Chief Police Officers, clearly set out the position with regard to shotgun security.

He made three main points:

1. The police would not have the resources to visit and inspect security in the homes of some 908,000 shotgun certificate holders. (The same points would, presumably, also apply to the proposal to transfer semi-autos and pump-action shotguns to Section 1. T.J.)

2. The police do not want to make the inspection of security a precondition to the grant of a shotgun certificate.

3. The police would want to see a provision in the legislation whereby people who, by negligence or failing to provide adequate security, allowed their shotguns to be stolen or fall into unauthorised hands, could be prosecuted.

The chief danger of a shotgun security system based on a condition on a shotgun certificate would be the latitude it would leave the police to interpret their powers, leading to a wide variation in decisions from force to force, misunderstanding and a worsening of relations between the police and shotgun certificate holders. Section 1 firearm certificate holders are well aware that the criteria for granting and renewing these certificates varies throughout the country, according to the whims of chief constables, some of whom choose to create their own conditions. There seems little reason to suppose that shotgun certificate holders, wishing to retain their semi-autos or pumps, would be treated in a different or more equable fashion, unless strict guidelines were laid down by the Home Office and adhered to by chief constables.

The White Paper suggests that a chief officer of police will have the power to refuse or revoke a certificate if security is inadequate. Security is a specialist subject and there is little doubt that if the police have to inspect the security arrangements of close on a million shotgun certificate holders, numerous officers will be involved with little or no knowledge of guns and firearms legislation. The result will be chaos, ill-feeling and an unnecessary increase in the burden of bureaucracy.

BASC, well aware of its responsibilities to its members and the shooting public, has for some considerable time laid heavy emphasis on shotgun security. Their leaflet, "Shotgun Safety Code", carries a section which demands that shooters keep shotguns and cartridges in separate safe places, preferably locked out of sight and emphasise that a proper security cabinet is ideal. Owners should also keep a separate record of serial numbers and photographs of guns.

BASC firmly recommends that a provision that the owner of a shotgun is responsible for its safe-keeping, failing which he is liable to prosecution, should be embedded in the Bill. This would be a clear, unequivocal statement, binding on all, and not subject to interpretation.

Good Reason

The balance of control where the granting of shotgun certificates is concerned will now shift, under the Bill, so that the police will have the power to refuse a certificate if they believe security arrangements are, in their view, inadequate or they believe the applicant does not have a good reason for possessing, purchasing or acquiring a shotgun.

Whilst this would appear to provide them with wide interpretative powers a clause in the Bill spells out a "good reason", namely: "if the gun is intended to be used for sporting or competition purposes or for shooting vermin". This is important as it acknowledges for the first time the roles played by shooting, both live and target, and enshrines them into the legislation.

One of the principle arguments put forward in favour of a "good reason" clause is that people are applying for shotgun certificates for self-defence and the defence of property. This, if it is a fact, is an alarming trend and reflects sadly on our society...*if it is a fact.*

It would be interesting to know what evidence is available to support this statement. If such applications have been made one would assume that the police would have refused them under the requirement of "public safety and the peace", with a final appeal available to the Courts. In other words, if applications are being made for shotgun certificates for reasons of self-defence the current legislation is perfectly capable of coping with the situation and no further amendments are required.

74

Whilst the Bill, as explained above, provides for "good reasons", it is another area which leaves the police in a position to refuse certificates, perhaps through misunderstanding or an over-zealous application of the rules.

Quite apart from sporting, competition shooting and vermin control, many people possess shotguns for their investment value rather than use, and as heirlooms to be passed on within a family. Many shotguns are extremely valuable, verging on works of art, and are collected with a view to realising their value rather than a desire to use them in the field.

Under section 43 of the White Paper, whilst the Government agrees that there would be little significant benefit gained in imposing arbitrary limits on the number of weapons which an individual may possess, recognising that competition shooters may require several, they state that where sporting guns are concerned: "...the Government feels it is best left to the police, drawing on guidance, to decide whether an application for a further firearm is supported by a good reason for possessing it. *This in itself represents a control on the accumulation of weapons."* (My italics T.J.)

In other words the police will be in a position to refuse applications if they choose to decide that an applicant does not need another gun. How to explain to a constable, lacking any knowledge of sporting shooting, that one needs a magnum 12-bore for wildfowling in addition to one's game gun, and perhaps an over-and-under for clays or that you wish to invest in a Best London gun or pair with no intention of use? All perfectly logical and reasonable to a shooting man, but perhaps a maze of misunderstanding for a policeman who may, and probably does, lack specialist knowledge or even has a bias against shooting.

Although the "good reason" requirement defines sporting shooting as one such in the Bill, this again can lead to misunderstanding and friction. Demands to justify an application on these grounds may be made in the form of written permission to shoot on land. Not every sportsman has his own shoot or ground and many rely on invitations or prefer to buy days on game shoots.

Land inspections may well follow, with territorial conditions written into the certificate. Untrained police may make capricious and uniformed decisions. This situation has in the past created enormous and unnecessary problems for firearm certificate holders and applicants due to the restrictive view applied by some constabularies when applying the Recommendations of the 1984 Working Party Report. However, this situation has now been resolved by the Home Office, ACPO and BSSC. It would be appalling if a similar situation arose with shotgun certificates.

75

Listing Shotguns on Certificates

This provision would appear to be singularly pointless though, doubtless, to a bureaucreatic mind it appears logical. Apparently it is intended that shotguns should be listed by serial number or description where there is no number, on a shotgun certificate.

However, as BASC have pointed out, the sheer administrative burden of acquiring the details of some 3 million shotguns would require the establishment of a large national registration and administration centre with all the attendant bureaucratic muddle. Such a register would have to be meticulously maintained if it were to have any value.

How, too, is it proposed that details of every one of the 3 million shotguns is obtained? Voluntary information is hardly likely to succeed so that one is led to presume that police will invoke section 46 of the Firearms Act, which allows power of search with a warrant, to seek entry to houses to obtain the information required.

What would be the purpose of such a register? Presumably to link stolen shotguns with those used in crime but as the police admit they have the greatest difficulty in tying firearms used in crime to those known to have been stolen it would seem a pointless exercise.

There is also the danger that this proposal on its own, or associated with the "good reason" clause, may result in guns being disposed of "underground" or into an illegal pool, if some people feel that they are going to be deprived of their guns.

The question of compensation is also one which is likely to create a considerable amount of ill-will and dissension. The Government refuses to pay compensation to owners of weapons which may now become prohibited. They agree that whilst there is no market for them in this country, dealers will be able to export them abroad.

Why, one wonders, is it acceptable that weapons, considered undesirable in this country, should be presumed admissible in other countries? Is there, too, not a great danger that these weapons will filter into the illegal terrorist pool?

This is, bluntly, careless thinking and merely reflects the entire approach to the construction of the Firearms (Amendment) Bill.

9
We Say...

John Anderton, Director of the British Association for Shooting & Conservation

Discussions about reforming the Firearms Act 1968 have been going on for at least 15 years. In 1973 the then Conservative Government produced a Green Paper on Firearms Controls which, through a concerted effort by all our friends, we got rid of. That Green Paper contained many of the proposals which we are now seeing resurrected in the current Firearms Bill as a result of Hungerford. The public has also become much more sensitive to the criminal use of firearms and also to the possibility that firearms could be used very dangerously in moments of civil protest. But even if the content of that Green Paper had reached the statute book, it would not have prevented Hungerford.

As soon as Hungerford happened, we knew straight away that two things would result. Firstly, public attitudes, whipped up by the media, towards the legitimate use and ownership of firearms would change dramatically; secondly there would be tensions built up between the different firearms owning publics, for example, the landed sporting interest in the shires game shooting and the various practical shooting disciplines which are identified with 'survivalism'.

As soon as the Home Secretary announced that the Government was seeking an urgent review of Firearms Law back at the end of August 1987, the BASC spoke out on behalf of the legitimate shotgun user. We recognised, of course, our place within the British Shooting Sports Council, which is the umbrella organisation for all shooting interests and disciplines but we felt that we had a major responsibility for our 90,000 plus members and over 1,000 affiliated clubs and registered syndicates. Indeed our membership makes up the largest single lobby group within the firearms owning community. We were also very much aware that our firearms department at the BASC is the only professional organisation of its kind and that it handles thousands of firearms regulation queries each year. Our firearms department has very wide practical experience, perhaps wider than any other institution in Britain, whether governmental, police or civilian. The BASC, as an Association, has a proven track record of sound and carefully considered advice. We felt that we had a very powerful need to be speaking out on behalf of the million strong firearms owning public.

Our first message was to applaud the Government's apparent intention not to rush into decisions which could have hidden repercussions. We welcomed the Minister's plan to consult fully with the shooting organisations. We deplore the fact that he failed to do so. What he has done in practice is to announce his intentions after they have been published, which is not a very constructive way to go about things. Possibly his mind was made up for him without heeding first-class knowledge or experience, i.e. the full facts!

In those early days, at the end of August, there was an avalanche of nonsense put out by the media (see Chapter 10) and, indeed, from self-styled experts on our 'own side', on the way firearms could be obtained and held by members of the public and what should be done. That was more than unfortunate and very unhelpful to our cause and the public interest. We stressed that Britain has the strictest rules on firearms ownership in Europe and we also went out of our way to underline the fact that we recognise the police take their responsibiliities very seriously indeed to make those regulations work. We also repeated the widely accepted view that the firearms-owning public, by definition, is the most law-abiding section of the community.

At that early stage the Home Secretary identified four critical points which he wanted the Home Office to consider:-

1. Banning semi-automatic weapons

2. Limiting the amount of ammunition kept in the home

3. The number of firearms on a certificate

4. Holding an amnesty for handing in unlicenced weapons

We considered that a total ban on all semi-automatic weapons, including pistols, would be disastrous for British shooting. They are essential for a broad section of competitive sport, including a large part of our Olympic team, not to mention a considerable number of .22 rim-fire rifles used in pest control. We are now able to welcome the fact that the Government has removed the .22 rim-fire weapons from further restriction. That is a plus point. On the question of the amount of ammunition kept in the home, we also took a very tough line and the Government has not moved on that point either. We welcome that, too.

We also took a tough line on the question of restricting the number of firearms on a certificate. We argued that different tasks require different types of firearm. On that point, too, the Government has not gone forword, which we regard as a victory for commonsense.

Following the Home Secretary's initial announcement there then ensued a period in which the BASC was very closely involved in discussions with Government departments, the Home Office itself, as well as our kindred organisations on the British Shooting Sports Council, discussing the issues and deciding the position the British shooting community and the BASC should take.

At the end of September the Home Secretary made a formal declaration of his main pillars of policy on which his proposals would be based. At that stage it was quite apparent that the Home Secretary was falling unduly under the influence of the Police Federation who have a history of being against the legitimate firearm user. The Police Federation were obviously failing to think through the implications of their advice. They were attempting to railroad additional restrictions on shotguns, which were not pertinent to an event such as Hungerford. At this time we made considerable play of the fact that a previous Home Secretary, Leon Brittan, had dismissed the types of proposals now under consideration by virtue of having accepted the argument that legislative restrictions have not stopped pistols being used in armed robberies far more than shotguns.

But the main emphasis of our assault on the Home Secretary's proposals was that they were dangerously vague and imprecise. Our fears have not be lessened on sight of the Bill. Indeed, they have increased, not least on account of the extraordinarily wide discretionary powers to be vested in Chief Officers of Police. We emphasised then, and we have not budged an inch from that view, that the proposals will not only fail to solve the problem of armed crime but they will do far-reaching damage to the interests of legitimate owners of firearms. The Home Secretary will find it extremely difficult to convert his proposals into effective and practical legislation. We feared then, and we fear now, that the proposals will undermine existing legislation and that would be a very bad thing for all concerned.

We also emphasised that the Home Secretary has placed himself at a distinct disadvantage through not availing himself of proper advice. The BASC has long called for a properly constituted advisory committee to assist the Home Secretary in this sort of deliberation. We find it quite inconceivable that he should go on groping in the dark, his path dimly lit by the limited advice of his own civil servants and distinctly misleading advice from the Police Federation, neither of which have the breadth of experience required. This is no way to tackle issues of the complexity raised by firearms legislation. It is a recipe for disaster and we fear for the future, and not least for the trust established with the police, which had greatly improved prior to August 1987.

At that time we heard, notwithstanding what the Home Secretary had promised earlier, that all pump-action and semi-automatic shotguns were to be treated as Part 1 firearms. We made the point that these shotguns are the most popular weapons for clay shooting world-wide and they are also widely used by wildfowlers and in pest control. They are particularly suitable for training purposes as they are tough and have a low recoil. We pressed the view that the Home Secretary would have to face up to a massive compensation bill if he wished to take such weapons out of private ownership. This whole question of compensation is still a matter of live debate, since these weapons are worth many thousands of pounds and it would be a disaster if they leaked on to the 'black market' in an uncontrolled manner.

The whole question of introducing a statutory safe keeping condition for shotguns when they are not in use is extremely thorny. This is not a new issue, it is one that has been in the background, under our very active consideration, for some time. But our view has always been that the evidence is quite clear on the matter. Although superficially attractive, such a measure would do nothing to hinder the armed criminal. There is already confusion in law as to when a weapon is not in use. We are pleased, however, to see that the Home Secretary will clarify this point to some degree. But our main point of concern is that such a proposal will be uninforceable or enforced arbitrarily by local police forces. We are, and have been, against the arbitrary exercise of ill-defined powers, whether on the part of the police or any other official body. It is just not the way we think a democracy should be run. We don't think that the Home Office and the Police Federation have given serious thought to the enormous extra burden that this proposal would mean for the 'bobby on the beat', who will have the task of checking up on where shotguns are kept. He will also face the antagonism of certain shotgun owners who may well resent the fact that the police have been given a statutory right of entry into their homes.

From that point onwards in September to the time when the Government published its White Paper on Firearms Reform at the beginning of December, the discussions continued with the Home

Office in particular, and also within the British Shooting Sports Council, as to how things should be handled. The BSSC appointed a public relations company to handle their press contacts and there has been a great deal of work in coordinating the different areas of the firearms lobby. The BASC itself had important meetings with ministers in its own right and as part of delegations from the BSCC. We also took a considerable amount of trouble to brief our parliamentary and political friends on the issues at stake and to explain our views.

As soon as the Government made known its precise proposals for legislation in the White Paper (Command 261) the Association's Council met and took the very important decision to mobilise the Association's membership to counter certain specific threats to legitimate shotgun users; in particular, on the question of pump-action and semi-automatic shotguns, and having a good reason for obtaining a shotgun certificate without defining what a good reason might be. On this point the Government has provided some welcome satisfaction. The Bill contains a definition of good reason which includes sport, and we welcome that fact. The BASC Council was also emphatic about the dangers of giving the police the right of entry into homes without a search warrant to inspect safe keeping arrangements, without defining what those arrangements might be. They felt that this was dangerously counter-productive and they gave their go-ahead for the Association to take a very tough stance on that issue. At that stage we were particularly concerned about the Government's unwillingness to provide financial compensation to those affected by the new legislation.

The Government published its Bill on December 17 in indecent haste after the White Paper which had appear on the 2nd. Notwithstanding the fact that the Government has moved a considerable way to meet, in part, the Association's suggestions and demands, we are still very much of the view that the Bill introduces areas of bureaucratic nightmare. It will do little to benefit the security of the community and much to create friction between the responsible firearms owner and the police.

The Bill has, in particular, focussed our attention on the question of registering individual shotguns on a certificate. Administratively, we feel that this is a nonsense, because if it is to make any sense at all it will have to be computerised centrally, and that will require a facility one quarter the size of the Vehicle Licencing Centre at Swansea. This will introduce an administrative burden on the 52 police firearms departments of horrendous dimensions, not to mention the very high level of unprecedented coordination and

LP—G

cooperation that would have to take place between the police forces and the central register, and the cooperation that would be required from the individual owners of shotguns. We just cannot see this idea working and believe it to be a non-starter. The final nail in its coffin is that it has also been tried in numerous other countries and dismissed.

This leads one to the question of discretionary powers to be given to Chief Officers of Police. There is no doubt that a minority of them have their own individual and idiosyncratic approaches. Nobody knows where they stand, least of all the responsible firearms owner. The introduction of vague measures of this kind will make things worse. The British institutions which exist to decide limitations on public rights are Parliament and the courts. For Parliament to opt out of its responsibilities and give these wide discretionary powers to the police is thoroughly bad. The proposals for firearms legislation must contain clear and unambiguous instructions to the police on the whole question of certification of firearms and security.

Finally, there is the foolish proposal to crack down on sporting pump-action and semi-auto shotguns, which we feel is totally unjustified. It will undoubtedly be deeply resented by the many thousands of owners. The proposals for legislation must be changed to ensure that shotguns commonly used for sporting purposes are not caught up in further restriction. This is a matter of simple error and injustice and I sincerely hope that this will indeed come about in the passage of the Bill through both Houses of Parliament.

In closing I would like to end on a broad and general point, namely that the Bill fails to recognise the complicated nature of firearms legislation. It makes no reference to the clear need for a ministerial advisory committee, something which we have been seeking for many, many years. If one had such a group of people able and willing to give sound advice and help thrash out practical solutions, we would be able to prevent the mess that we now have. The legitimate sporting firearms public would be 100 per cent behind the Government and the police in seeking to ensure that the least possible opportunity is given to criminals to have access to firearms. There would be every prospect of looking to an effective administration of our firearms regulations which could go some way to ensure that tragedies of the type that we witnessed at Hungerford, never occur again. But, was Ryan a criminal or a man who suddenly lost his reason?

We must bring about these changes before the Bill becomes law.

There is, looking to the future, an important part for legitimate and responsible firearms owners to play – whether for sporting purposes, for target shooting or pest control, shooting provides excellent discipline for the young. The controlled and safe use of firearms is a benefit to society. We must ensure that the people who wish to avail themselves of this right are able to do so without bureaucratic interference. I can put my hand on my heart and say that BASC has done, is doing and will continue to do, everything it possibly can to ensure that freedom is sustained and promoted and made stronger in the weeks, months and years ahead.

John Hopkinson, Director of the British Field Sports Society – *Taped Interview*

I think that some quite useful and responsible decisions have been taken, on the other hand there is no doubt a number of the measures have been constructed for cosmetic reasons, or appear to have been taken for cosmetic reasons, rather than for real increases in the public safety so that the people who suffer are actually the legitimate weapons holders.

We understand why the Government feels they have to do this and we understand the feeling in the country is that they should take some form of firm action. Yet it's difficult for us to explain that we thought the previous regulations were pretty good. But I think it is worth highlighting, and it is a point the Home Secretary made, that there is a growing number of weapons being held in urban areas for purposes which, strictly speaking, have nothing to do with sporting or target shooting. This is what he is concerned about, and there is no doubt in our minds that were some action not to be taken to control that spread, eventually we would get very much tougher legislation because of the increasing rise in the use of weapons in crime and in defence by people who possess weapons not for the reasons most sporting people possess them.

That is where we, the sporting public, have also got to take into account another aspect. This legislation is likely to be with us for 15 to 20 years and it is better to accept some form of legislation now and hope we can keep it like that, rather than have some draconian measure in three or four years time which could well occur if there were a continuing spread of weapons into the urban areas and held by individuals for no reason connected with sport.

An important aspect

One point that is particularly interesting is that in this Bill the

Government have gone to great trouble to ensure that sporting shooting is included as a good reason for possessing a gun. This is probably the single most important aspect contained in the Bill because it is in direct opposition to the Labour Party spokesman's view that the shooting of a pheasant was not necessarily a good reason to have a shotgun. So I think that aspect, where sporting shooting people are concerned, is a very significant thing in that it enshrines in the Firearms Bill the fact that there is a good reason for sporting shooting.

Security

One of the principal problems not covered in the Bill is the question of security. It would appear that security is going to be covered in the Rules and to be applied to the provision of a shotgun certificate. In other words you will have to show you have adequate security before you obtain a certificate. We believe that if that decision is left entirely to the police this sets up a confrontational aspect between the shooting public and the police, something we wish to avoid because we think the police are doing a good job and we want to help them do it.

What we believe is that there should be a clause in the Bill which lays down that anyone who wishes to possess a shotgun is responsible for the security of that gun and that the guidance given, the Code of Practice, should be an agreed Code of Practice and should be put together by an Expert Consultative Committee. Such a Committee should consist of police, the Home Office officials and the firearms users. We are saddened that that provision is not included in the Bill.

In simplistic terms we shall be saying to the Government that we wish the Rules to be made under an Affirmative Order and this is the Amendment we shall seek to get in the Committee stage. That means that anything that goes into the Rules will have to be debated. Therefore, in the Report stage of the Bill we ought to be able to raise the security issue so that at least we can get it discussed.

No common policy

The thing that I'd like to stress is that it is not that we don't trust or dislike the police – some people would say that it's not our line – we think the problem lies with the system of 52 chief constables, all with different views, so that it's extremely difficult for us to carry responsible members with us when they're all writing in saying, oh, my chief constable won't do this when another chief constable may have very different rules and agree. It makes it very difficult for us to be seen to be supportive of the police and yet try to help people obtain firearm certificates when, in fact, there is no common interpretation of policy. We think it is up to the Government to lay down the policy and full guidelines for its interpretation. The existence of an Expert Consultative Committee would greatly help in this respect.

Semi-autos and pump-action guns

As far as semi-autos and pump-action shotguns are concerned and the proposal that they be placed on a Part 1 firearms basis, obviously we are very concerned about this. These guns are used in sporting shooting, vermin control and clay pigeon shooting; what's more they are an extremely good medium for teaching youngsters and women to shoot. They are sensible weapons to have for sporting purposes. Having said that, the Government don't intend to ban them, but to put stricter conditions on them and many of the people who have these shotguns also have firearms certificates. So in some cases there will be no problem, but by the same token many people will find that a problem does arise and they're going to have to go through the rigmarole of obtaining firearms certificates.

The BFSS wanted to get over this by a restriction of two cartridges in the magazine since it was the volume of fire which concerned the Government rather than the action of the weapon. If the gun can be adapted or restricted to hold two cartridges in the magazine, such guns should remain on a shotgun certificate. All other shotguns, with a higher rate or capacity of fire, should go on a firearms certificate. As far as the Browning 2-shot semi-auto is concerned, and there must be quite a few still in use, we can see no problem. They are no more lethal than a double-barrelled shotgun.

The argument for putting a semi-automatic on a Part 1 basis is an unusual one, because a man with a box of 25 cartridges using a conventional double will actually get off more cartridges, in shorter space of time, than he will with a semi-automatic.

Shotgun certificates

Where the grant of certificates is concerned the onus in the Bill has now swung on to the applicant to prove a requirement, a situation which gives the police considerable latitude, but we're hoping we can swing that back in the committee stage. There is no doubt that the Government is willing to listen to proposals put to them and has gone some way to meeting our concern in Clause 3 (1B).

Semi-auto rifles

As far as self-loading rifles are concerned the BFSS point of view is that they are not weapons which are required for field sports. A very small number are used for sport and we would not go down the line specifically of making a song-and-dance about them. We don't think they are a good idea for stalking.

There are, of course, a number of field sportsmen who use semi-auto rifles for target shooting and by placing them in section 5, the so-called prohibited category, they are not strictly speaking totally banned. They are in fact put in a section where the Home Secretary has to give the authority and make the regulations. It's not left to the individual police forces. It seems to us that there is still the ability for the Home Secretary to make provision for the use of those weapons. I'd like to see a provision for their use for target purposes within the Bill.

As far as visitors from abroad are concerned we don't see a problem. Most visitors who come to shoot here don't do so on the spur of the moment. The current regulations have, in fact, been simplified and cover shotguns which they didn't do before. In the main we think there is little harm in this provision.

Lord Swansea, Chairman of the British Shooting Sports Council – *Taped Interview*

Semi-auto rifles

As far as these weapons are concerned the NRA does not organise competitions for self-loading rifles, except for the Services and they, of course, will carry on with those competitions. We do know, however, that there are quite a lot of people in clubs who don't take part in NRA competitions – they belong to provincial clubs and don't come to Bisley – who enjoy ordinary target shooting at their clubs with self-loading rifles. That is quite separate and distinct from the practical shooters who will really be the most affected by this legislation. The ordinary club shooter who finds himself unable to possess a self-loading rifle will not be too concerned about that; he'll dispose of his rifle by what ever means he can and carry on with an orthodox bolt-action rifle. But it is the practical shooters who are most at risk and their sport, which is now an international one, is going to be severely affected. They'll be at a considerable disadvantage, as they'll only be able to participate with bolt-action rifles.

Right from the beginning we have been trying to persuade the Home Office that there is a legitimate use for rifles of this sort. Normally a provision to own section 5 weapons is restricted to dealers who operate overseas and weapons in that category are normally never allowed to be possessed by individuals. We are trying to persuade the Government there is scope for self-loading rifles for perfectly ordinary target shooting as distinct from the practical shooting aspect.

The type of rifle used by Ryan, the Kalashnikov and others like it, is a close-range assault rifle with an effective range of about 3-400 metres, whereas the ordinary target shooter may wish to carry on his sport up to 1,000 metres for which the assault-type of rifle is quite unsuitable.

Semi-auto and pump-action shotguns

Another very important proposal is to bring semi-auto and pump-action shotguns under Section 1 procedure and that will very seriously affect clay target shooters and others who use a shotgun for wildfowling and rough shooting. This type of gun is more preferred by women and people with a disability due to the reduced recoil.

Security

As far as security for shotguns is concerned one cannot reasonably object to this proposal. Most people are prepared to take any reasonable precautions to keep their shotgun in a safe place, especially if it has some intrinsic value.

Memorandum of Guidance

Unfortunately, many chief constables have widely differing ideas about the interpretation of the present Act. The Home Office recognises that a chief constable has discretion in his own parish, very wide discretion. Now the chief constable says that he is bound by the Home Office Memorandum of Guidance, so the shooter is in a pig-in-the-middle situation, he just can't win.

During the past year or so the Home Office have been revising the Memorandum of Guidance and they took us into consultation on it. They told us that whereas up till now it had been a private document it would now be made public, so we were consulted and helped in its drafting. There was one section which was still in draft stage, but of course the whole thing has gone out of the window because of the event of the past few months. No doubt a new Memorandum of Guidance will have to be worked out from scratch following the passing of this new Bill. We still hope it will be in the public domain and we will again be consulted. We may then be in a position to say to a chief constable exceeding his powers, you can't do that!

Expert Consultative Committee

We are also doing our level best to persuade the Home Office that an Expert Consultative Committee is desirable, but so far we have met with some resistance. The last time we met the Home Secretary he said that if such a Committee was formed we would have to bring in all sorts of bodies on it, such as the RSPCA, the League Against Cruel Sports, Uncle Tom Cobley and all. But the current Firearms Act and the proposed Bill are concerned with the ownership of firearms and shotguns and not the manner in which they are used. That is a point we hope to press strongly during the passage of this Bill through Parliament and we hope very much we can persuade the Government to accept that principle and to establish an Expert Consultative Committee.

Christopher Brunker, Christie's Firearms Department

As the representative of the Gun Trade Association on the British Shooting Sports Council, I have had privileged access to the current firearms debate. Though I draw on this experience, the following assessment is entirely personal.

I believe that the Firearms Bill, currently before Parliament, is flawed in principle and in detail. It has little (if any) relevance to crime, but is a real threat to a variety of legitimate interests. I also fear that the extent and seriousness of this threat is not fully appreciated by many of those directly affected. This is probably most common among those who own only traditional shotguns.

However, the most disturbing aspect of this whole issue is what it reveals about the way government works. Firearms are a subject of which I have some knowledge and experience, and it is frightening to discover the lack of understanding upon which decisions in government are made. Firearms and their control are a complex matter. Lack of expertise in relation to them is not confined to government, but those entrusted with power have a duty to use it wisely. This they cannot hope to do if they do not grasp the fundamentals. There is a clear need for a permanent, statutory expert body to advise on firearms legislation and on the administration of firearms law, but the Home Office has consistently resisted this idea.

All this is sad for the shooting community, who are unfairly penalised, and for the police, who are increasingly required to act beyond their resources and competence. However, the implications are much wider and I am left with the alarming proposition that all government may be conducted with a comparable lack of objectivity and expertise.

Keith Murray, Director of the Clay Pigeon Shooting Association

It had been anticipated for a number of years that some changes in the existing Firearms Acts were going to be made. Well informed sources within the shooting organisations were monitoring the situation and ready to nullify or minimise the impact of any unnecessary changes on the legitimate gun owner.

The Hungerford massacre changed all that. The present Government, given a mandate to curb the growth in the 'lawless society', responded as only political minds can, by proposing to restrict the rights of the 'lawful society'.

It was a popular move – one opinion on the radio stated that *all* gun owners were evil – and with the media in support, the facts of the case, that a deranged man had murdered law-abiding citizens was transferred to the weapon by which he perpetrated the outrage. Thus guns were to be restricted.

Pressure by a good number of CPSA members was for opposing *all* further restrictions on gun ownership. After considerable heart-searching and alert to the "tip of the iceberg" syndrome, it was decided that the CPSA must assume a responsible attitude as far as possible and consult with sister organisations and the Home Office to allow the legitimate and responsible sportsman to continue to enjoy his pastime without undue hindrance.

The present form of the "Firearms Act 1968 – Proposals for Reform" still unnecessarily curtails the clay pigeon shooter and whilst there is concern for a good many of areas covered by the proposals, three are potentially dangerous to the sport.

First, placing of semi-automatic shotguns under Section 1 of the Act. Many of our shooters, particularly the less able, ladies and juniors, use these weapons mainly because they absorb a great deal of recoil. Any restriction on such weapons would certainly be a blow to many present users, some of whom might have to give up shooting.

Since the restriction is to be imposed because of the gun's ability to hold more than two cartridges (as is normal in a standard shotgun), a modification and time available to implement the modification would seem to be the simplest solution.

Secondly, gun security. It is certainly not unreasonable to ask a shotgun owner to keep the weapon secure – but what is security? Police have different requirements on this and a guide to chiefs of police rationalising the requirements would be a practical and constructive solution.

Thirdly, compensation. Any surrendered or newly prohibited

weapons would be taken without compensation. The proposals state that it would be unjust to ask the taxpayer to pay the bill for any compensation! To me, it is unfair that goods which I bought legally and at considerable expense in one year should be declared illegal and become my total loss in another year.

The CPSA is striving, and will continue to strive, to do all in its power to ensure that the sport of clay pigeon shooting can be enjoyed in future years. The proposals, at the time of going to press, are just that. It is not too late to take individual action, if you have not yet done so. Write to the Home Office and your own Member of Parliament and tell him or her of your concern – it is your sport!

10
The Media Says...

The Press reaction to the Hungerford and Bristol killings was predictable. Yards of emotional, hysterical clap-trap filled the columns and opinion pages of every newspaper throughout the land. Editors and leader writers overnight became firearms experts, whilst each and anyone with a reason, however misplaced, to fear guns in whatever guise, took the opportunity to leap on the now rolling bandwagon.

It became a wonderful chance for town to attack the country and for gratuitous swipes at land owners and the 'gun lobby'. Those opposed to shooting for sport dashed into print to condemn every aspect of guns and shooting. Logic and commonsense flew out of the window, to be replaced by bigotry and bitterness. The ugly face of prejudice and envy was quick to show itself.

As usual certain elements of the Press maintained par for the course by displaying their total ignorance of firearms and guns, semi-autos and burst-fire weapons, live shooting and target shooting, with some amazingly confused and illogical pronouncements. Fortunately, these were countered by commonsense statements from the BASC, the BFSS and the gun trade, whilst many private individuals put forward the case for shooting.

The following is a cross-section of Press reporting, comment and readers' letters:

Southern Evening Echo, Southampton. Aug. 24. Reader's letter.

In the wake of a spate of mindless outbursts in recent weeks the Echo Comment headed "Gun Law" must come as no surprise.

In the past I spent nine enjoyable years rifle and pistol shooting, including two years trading as a firearms dealer. As I now have no connection with shooting in any form my comments come from outside the "determined lobby" mentioned in your article.

The record of the licenced shooter in the country needs no close examination to confirm the findings of previous reviews which have concluded that firearms in private ownership under the present laws are not a threat to public safety, nor does it really need me to repeat the overwhelming feeling of shooters that the present penalties for all forms of violent crime are a positive incentive to the illegal use of firearms and should be reviewed urgently.

The real problem is that the shooter, being part of a minority interest, attracts the attentions of the worst sort of journalism. The claim made that mass shootings are common in the U.S.A. is a typical example. Not only are such incidents rarer than the level of gun ownership would lead us to expect but they are far less common than the incidents of mass violence reported by your own paper with monotonous regularity but not attracting editorial comment because they involve sharp or blunt intruments and motor vehicles.
John C. Evans, Southampton.

Today, London. Sept. 23. **The Voice of Today**.
A young man, when asked what the American constitution meant to him in the year of its bicentennial, said: "It means my dad and I can carry guns."

To us in Britain, civil liberties have less to do with the right to carry weapons of self-defence (or murder) and more to do with the right to live without fear of being shot.

Nevertheless it is the American attitude that finds echoes in the Home Secretary's decision to ban some – but not ALL – guns. In making this half-hearted proposal, he bows to the gun lobby of landowners and so-called field sportsmen.

There are obvious ironies in our concern for the rights of nature and man. We are forbidden to pick cowslips, but we are not forbidden to own an armoury of semi-automatic machine-guns.

… In the name of those who were cruelly slaughtered because the right to own guns is somehow more sacred than the right to remain alive, we must ban ALL guns and we must ban them NOW. There is no half-way house between life and death.

This is a superb example of emotive non-thinking, linking non-sequitors and making a bold, brash appeal which will appeal to an ignorant public. The inference is that "so-called" field sportsmen (why so-called? They either are or are not field sportsmen) and landowners use semi-automatic rifles (or machine-guns) to slaughter wildlife – vide the 'rights of nature and man'.

Daily Telegraph, extract from 'Hurd's Gun Law' by Lin Jenkins. Sept. 23
… The gun lobby maintains that Hurd's proposals ignore the statistics that show that hardly any weapons used in violent crime are licenced in the first place. "Just because of a single abberration, our civil liberties are to be removed," said McAllister (Jim McAllister,

NRA) "The problem has been blown out of all proportion. Only eight people died of gunshot wounds last year, and that includes suicides. Whatever you do, you cannot legislate against the likes of Michael Ryan."

However, Leslie Curtis of the 120,000-strong Police Federation, believes that Hurd's measures do not go far enough. He wants safe storerooms at gun clubs so members would not be allowed to take their guns home. The Federation will continue to lobby for such measures, while those who use guns will continue their battle to dis-associate their ranks from the actions of a maniac on a quiet after-noon in a sleepy market town...

The **Daily Mirror** was quick to jump on the band-wagon. On Sept. 23 it ran a front-page attack on pump-action shotguns with a story about two brothers *"blasted with a pump-action shotgun in a quiet street"*. The man *"loosed off eight shots from a single-barrelled gun, leaving smoking shells littering the pavement."*

In their Comment the **Mirror** claim: *He (Douglas Hurd) will make it harder, legally, to own pump-action shotguns. He should totally ban those as well. There can be no conceivable reason for anybody needing such a deadly weapon.*

On the same date the **Daily Express** ran the same story. There was however a subtle difference. In this case: *A man with a pump action double-barrel shotgun blasted two men in a quiet suburban street last night... The gunman had fired his weapon five times...*

So we had a pump-action in one story firing eight shots, in another five shots and also acquiring an extra barrel!

By October **Today** had slightly mollified its tone. Now, instead of a call to ban all guns, on October 15 it proposed: *These steps are essential: It must be made illegal to keep a gun at home. Certificates must only be issued after the most stringent vetting. The sportsmen and farmers who pass the test must keep their guns in police-control-led armouries when they are not in use.*

The gun lobby will squeal, of course. But let them squeal to their hearts' content. Saving lives is far more important than the right to pot clay pigeons.

Amidst all the affected piety and the humbug were to be found shafts of commonsense:

Yorkshire Evening Press, Oct. 30. Reader's letter.
Yet another editorial swipe at the shooting public. On the same page, a column by John Potts in like vein.

None of you appears to know the difference between a Smith and Wesson and a Black and Decker, but by inserting a "semi-automatic" here and an "arsenal" there, you feign some knowledge of the subject.

For your information, nearly all target pistols used in competition up to Olympic level are semi-automatic, as are many rifles and shotguns used by gamekeepers and sportsmen. I would dispute that this type of weapon is any more dangerous than a manually operated one.

Every morning the papers are full of horrible murders, hardly any of them involving firearms. Anyone who thinks the banning of guns, knives or whatever will have the slightest effect is either deluding himself or is a journalist trying to delude others.
J.C. Smith, York Guns, York.

Meanwhile The League Against Cruel Sports, never slow to miss an opportunity, seized the occasion to run a campaign to ban all guns through national advertising and a letters campaign.

Sample letter. **Feltham Chronicle**, Middx. Nov. 19.

The time has come for a ban on all guns, including shotguns. There are less than one million private citizens holding shotguns, the only excuse for most being a desire to shoot wildlife for the sheer pleasure of killing.

Is their right to shoot wildlife more sacred than the right of the police and public to stay alive? Shotguns were invented and permitted for this so-called sport, but hundreds of people have been murdered by these weapons and they have been used in thousands of armed robberies.

But for bloodsports, it is doubtful that any private citizen would be allowed to possess any gun. Rural residents have to suffer the noise, even on Sundays, and 3,000 tons of toxic lead shot is spread over our countryside every year. Despite all of that, the totally selfish shooting minority is determined to wreck the already inadequate proposals put forward by the Government.

The police, the public, The Association of County Councils, and conservationists want controls on shotguns as well as controls on self-loading weapons and right is on our side.

The League Against Cruel Sports has mounted a national petition calling on the Government to ban all guns for those used by people who need them in their employment (sic).

The guns used for target and clay pigeon shooting should be kept

in maximum security at the shooting club premises...
Richard Course, Executive Director, LACS.

The BFSS and the BASC were quick to answer through a national letter campaign.

Sample letter. **Bexhill-on-Sea Observer**, Nov. 19.

The campaign mounted by the League Against Cruel Sports to ban all guns is a shameless attempt by this pressure group to exploit the tragedy at Hungerford at the expense of tens of thousands of responsible gun owners in this country.

In the interests of accuracy, I would like to make the following points. In recent years the number of burglaries has increased dramatically yet the number of weapons stolen has remained much the same, a few hundred every year. As a percentage of the total number of legally-held firearms, it is a tiny amount when you consider that nearly a million people hold shotgun certificates. Criminals do not apply for gun licences.

To imply that gun owners pose a threat to wildlife, as the League attempts to do, is the reverse of the truth. All responsible conservation bodies accept that the millions of pounds spent annually on sporting shooting makes a vital contribution to the well-being of all wildlife through the creation and preservation of habitat.

Shooting organisations are actively involved in sponsoring research in many different areas. For example the work of the Game Conservancy on the decline of the English partridge has produced results of inestimable value to wildlife. At this point it is fair to ask what contribution the League Against Cruel Sports has made to practical conservation.

Finally I must stress the value that shooting makes to the hard-pressed rural economy. It has a turnover of some £200 million a year and the incomes of thousands of people depend on it.
John Hopkinson, Director, BFSS.

Sample letter. **Swindon Evening Advertiser**, Nov. 16.

The recent letter writing and advertising campaign instigated by the League Against Cruel Sports, has proved that the organisation is not averse to using such tragic incidents as Hungerford to achieve their own aims and ambitions. Such action is to be deplored by all right minded citizens.

Mr Richard Course, the LACS Director, states that "guns" are used by criminals in the furtherance of their illegal actions and,

*indeed this is true. But these weapons are illegally held and no
amount of legislation will control their use. No criminal will ever
adhere to lawful regulations limiting possession and use of guns, pistols or rifles. This is evident from the fact that the weapon most commonly used in crime is the handgun – the most difficult weapon to
obtain legally, as has been the case since 1920!*

*The Home Secretary has stated many times that "A tightening of
firearms legislation is no guarantee against tragedy" – a fact that is all
too obvious to anyone who cares to give the matter serious thought.*

*The League do a grave disservice to over a million legitimate users
of "guns" by using an advertisement which seeks to link armed criminals with lawful users. Many people would consider this to be verging on libel.*

*The only way to curtail the illegal use of guns is for the courts to use
the full weight of existing legislation and thereby help create an effective deterrent.*

J. McKay, BASC.

The Government's decision not to pay compensation to owners
whose weapons are proscribed under the new legislation and their
suggestion that owners will be able to sell such weapons to gun
dealers who, in turn, can dispose of them abroad, came in for some
considerable fire.

In a **Sunday Telegraph** article, Dec. 20 Jamie Dettmer, Political
Correspondent wrote: *An arsenal of weapons at knock-down
prices, which could fall into the hands of terrorists, will be released
by the Government's Firearms Bill, according to Common Market
countries. European countries are to protest to Mrs Thatcher over
the way Britain is planning its curb on sophisticated and high-pow-
ered weapons after the decision by Mr Hurd, the Home Secretary,
not to compensate gun owners whose firearms are prohibited.*

*They will tell the Prime Minister that British owners must not be
encouraged to sell their prohibited weapons on the international gun
market.*

*… Mr Roy Hattersley, the Shadow Home Secretary, joined in the
condemnation of the Government's plans and accused Mr Hurd of
"holding an irresponsible sale". "I am concerned by the Government's encouragement of the sale of deadly weapons at what will
inevitably be cheap prices on the international market," he said.
"There is every possibility that these weapons might be sold to people
who could use them for violent or terrorist activity which could spill
back over in Britain."*

The Irish, Dutch and West German Governments are known to be highly anxious about Britain's plans. A spokesman for the West German embassy said last night, "We would be worried about these guns going on to the black market." An Irish official described the move as "a very dangerous and disturbing development."

However, the Home Office is emphatic that the sale will not pose any security risk.

Perhaps the final word should come from the equally emphatic pen of Auberon Waugh's **Sunday Telegraph** column.

I have written already about the White Paper Firearm Act 1968, Proposals for reform, which is Mr Hurd's response to the Hungerford massacre, pointing out that while its proposals threaten the maximum possible amount of nuisance to Britain's 840,00 legitimate shotgun owners (the correct figure is, in fact, 908,000. T.J.), *they will do nothing to prevent criminals acquiring guns illegally, and nothing to prevent legitimate owners going berserk, as is occasionally bound to happen even with kitchen knives.*

Another objection is the degree of discretion allowed Chief Constables on whether to issue a licence or not. This might have worked when Chief Constables were more or less anonymous public servants, but with the new race of vulgarian exhibitionists – Sussex, Nottingham and Manchester are only the noisiest; several have questioned whether the public has any right to own sporting weapons at all – it will produce appalling anomalies between police authorities. It would be a dreadful thing if we were forced to decide where to live by the complexion of the local government authority, the local and education health authorities, and the local Chief Constable.

Government's job is to keep local Napoleons in their place, not to give them greater powers.

Mr Hurd should know about this, because he has already fallen foul of the very Firearms Act of 1968 which he now seeks to replace by something altogether more oppressive. In 1975 he was fined £5 for possessing two shotguns without a certificate.

Turning to section 41 of the White Paper, I see that "the maximum penalty for possessing a shotgun without a certificate is being raised to bring it into line with the same offence in respect of firearms (on indictment, three years imprisonment, or a fine, or both)".

In fact Hurd had simply forgotten to renew his certificate – something which might happen to any of us in the general proliferation of permits, licences, NI cards and parking tickets. Is three years imprisonment really a suitable punishment for neglecting one of these idiotic bits of paper?

LP—H

Post Script

On January 8, 1988 **Today**, determined to keep the fire blazing, ran a story covering the appalling shooting of a teacher by a 16-year-old pupil. Fortunately, although severely wounded in the face, the man was not fatally injured.

It was, however, seeen by **Today** as a perfect New Year opportunity to continue their attack on legitimate shotgun owners. This time the angle was children.

"Scandal of the shotgun 8-year-olds" screamed the headline. *"2,000 young fingers on the trigger"* ran a sub-head. It was the usual mixture of muddled semi-fact and emotive reporting.

Sample: *Children as young as eight are using shotguns regularly and perfectly legally. They are among an estimated 2,000-plus youngsters, mostly living in farming areas, licenced to blast away at live game or artificial targets. Hundreds more simply borrow guns from fathers or uncles and head off for the fields and woods without bothering about legal niceties.*

After this emotional and wholly unsupported statement, **Today** did at least have the grace to print a comment from Keith Murray, CPSA Director, who pointed out: *"Safety is drummed into our young members from the word go. We regularly hold courses to show children just how dangerous guns can be. When they see the impact of a shotgun cartridge on a plastic bottle of water they suddenly realise guns can do the most awful damage to people."*

In the same issue the **Today** leader reiterated its call for all guns to be locked securely away: *The right answers are clear. No gun licences should be issued to anyone under 17. And all guns must be kept locked in secure police amouries from which they can only be taken for specified reasons and precisely defined periods of time. It's no use the gun lobby throwing up its hands and bleating yet again – "It's not guns that kill, it's people." But their freedom to have guns is secondary to our freedom to stay alive. We can't keep finger-tip control over people who may suddenly and unpredictably go berserk. But we can control the guns they use to kill and maim innocent people. Which is what the Government must make up its mind to do right now...*

Quite apart from the curious use of grammar, it is a superb piece of non-think journalism. Appeal to the lowest common denominator and somewhere along the line you are bound to get it right. It was typical of the garbage churned out by certain elements of Fleet Street. Neither constructive nor helpful, but simply knee-jerk reaction to a situation with an eye on circulation.

One could query the figure of 2,000 youngsters. From whence did they arrive at this figure? On what evidence do they support the statement that hundreds borrow guns from fathers and uncles? Note the use of the word "blast" at live game instead of "shoot".

It was all symptomatic of the ignorance surrounding guns and shooting, a vein of prejudice which has invariably been a feature of Fleet Street. Aware of their smoke-filled, booze-laden reputation the Grub Street journalists have always taken a special delight in annoying or torturing the countryside and its inhabitants, especially if there is the slightest smell of class or social hatred to be stirred up.

Relevant Addresses

British Association for Shooting and Conservation (BASC)
    Marford Mill
    Rossett
    Wrexham
    Clwyd   LL12 0HL
    Telephone: (0244) 570881

Shooting Sports Trust
    Mediterranean Shooting Supplies Ltd
    P.O. Box 7
    Evesham   WR11 6JA
    Telephone: (0386) 3654

British Field Sports Society (BFSS)
    59 Kennington Road
    London SE1 7PZ
    Telephone: (01) 928 4742

Clay Pigeon Shooting Association (CPSA)
    107 Epping New Road
    Buckhurst Hill
    Essex   IG9 5TQ
    Telephone: (01) 505 6221

Gun Trade Association
    Fairbourne Cottage
    Bunny Lane
    Timsbury
    Nr. Romsey
    Hants   SO5 0PG
    Telephone: (0794) 68443

Game Conservancy
    Burgate Manor
    Fordingbridge
    Hants   SP6 1EF
    Telephone: (0425) 52381

British Shooting Sports Council
    115 Salter Lane
    Sheffield   SE11 8YR
    Telephone: (0742) 585974